MAGDA
My Journey

MAGDA WIERZYCKA

PENGUIN BOOKS

Magda: My Journey

Published by Penguin Books

an imprint of Penguin Random House South Africa (Pty) Ltd

Reg. No. 1953/000441/07

The Estuaries No. 4, Oxbow Crescent, Century Avenue, Century City, 7441

PO Box 1144, Cape Town, 8000, South Africa

www.penguinrandomhouse.co.za

Penguin
Random House
South Africa

First published 2022

1 3 5 7 9 10 8 6 4 2

Publication © Penguin Random House 2022

Text © Magda Wierzycka 2022

PUBLISHER: Marlene Fryer

MANAGING EDITOR: Robert Plummer

EDITOR: Bronwen Maynier

PROOFREADER: Alice Inggs

COVER DESIGNER: Ryan Africa

TYPESETTER: Monique van den Berg

Set in 11.5 pt on 16.5 pt Adobe Garamond Pro

Printed by **novus print**, a division of Novus Holdings

MIX
Paper from
responsible sources
FSC® C022948

ISBN 978 1 77609 666 4 (print)

ISBN 978 1 77609 667 1 (ePub)

This book is dedicated to my grandmother, Helunia Getreu, whose extra-ordinary courage and strength, and absolute determination to make the most of life despite the fate that befell her family, have inspired me to become who I am today. She was the person who told me, when I was still a child, that I must strive to be the best at everything I do. Her memory lives on through this book.

Contents

Preface

TAKING RISKS SEEMS TO BE in my blood. Perhaps it is my history as a refugee from communist Poland, my early experiences in aggressively male-dominated corporates, the lessons I learnt while building my own company, or my natural propensity to strive for justice at all costs. I came to that realisation while I was shuttered in a hotel in London for a week in 2017, trawling through over five hundred thousand emails documenting over five years of corruption and theft in South Africa, perpetrated by three brothers who had entangled the then president, Jacob Zuma, in a web of deceit that ultimately ruined the country, deprived many of livelihoods and education, and eventually and tangibly plunged South Africa into darkness as the country's electricity provision infrastructure started to fail.

As I researched WikiLeaks and other distribution strategies designed to democratise the information in my possession as soon as possible to protect those who brought it to me, as well as my family, I knew I had crossed an invisible line. I was no longer just a vocal anti-corruption business leader in South Africa. I had become part of something larger and darker, a journey that ultimately brought me into contact with state security agencies in South Africa and other countries, albeit the former not in a positive way. I knew that the information was dangerous and had to be distributed to disarm it.

Taking a day off to fly to Sweden to meet with a journalist from the International Consortium of Investigative Journalists proved to be a fruitless exercise as he was not interested in the story. I could either rely on others who planned to distribute the information over a lengthy timeline which would have compromised everyone, or take matters into my own hands. As always, I opted to act. As controversial as that decision remains, I firmly believe it was the right one. My life changed in 2017, but I do not regret anything that has happened since. I would not have it any other way and, faced with the same choices, I would do it all again.

I wondered at first why I would embark on writing a book at this stage of my life, beyond it being a vanity project. I have, however, been persuaded that I have a story to tell. It is a story that is meant to inspire those who follow in my footsteps, young people entering the workforce with ambition and drive who are struggling to achieve their full potential. At a very naive twenty-three, when I began my career, I did so unarmed for the battles I would have to fight. Twenty-eight years later, I bear many battle scars, but I am better armed and have developed a skill set that I wish I'd had when I started out. I know that there are still battles to be fought, and they are going to be tough, but I now deal with them differently, confident in the knowledge that at least I know what my own weaknesses are and how to manage them in adversity.

In this book, I have relied on a few studies and the views of pioneers who came before me to make some pertinent points. As an actuary, I like to support postulations with real scientific data. I have also relied on a few of my own previously published opinion pieces, articles and speeches, going back to 2008, to give you a glimpse into my ideas and thoughts in the past, many of which remain unchanged today.

I often ask myself if I have won anything for women in terms of my career in the financial services industry, and whether I have shattered any corporate glass ceilings. It is a difficult question to answer. When I look at it through the lens of purely financial success and building up a company worthy of a listing on a stock market, such as the Johannesburg Stock Exchange, then the answer is undoubtedly yes. But I achieved that success by stepping away from the traditional corporate world, with its politics and ladders, and by forging my own path. I stepped away not by choice, but because I was forced out. Eventually, it was easier to build my own house with lofty ceilings than try to break through the various glass ceilings that women in the traditional corporate world confront. So I am left wondering, was I truly a success in this regard or rather a failure of sorts?

On my journey I have encountered many people. Some have been incredible and some not. This story is not an exposé of anyone, although in places it might feel like one. I walked away from every encounter, good or bad, with more weapons and tools. At the time, some confrontations were deeply traumatic, and I carry the effects with me to this day, but I do believe they have made me a better and wiser person. I try to not repeat that behaviour in my own life, but instead pass on my lessons to others. A friend who has known me for twenty-eight years and witnessed my battles warned me to not come across as being bitter. That is the wise counsel I tried to keep in mind as I wrote this story.

I am also acutely aware that successful women today remain deeply polarising figures. It is enough to look at Theresa May, whose Brexit plan, initially discarded, was ultimately implemented once she was removed from power, and Hillary Clinton, who unquestionably would have been a better president than Donald Trump, to know that ultimately little has changed in the world and that women still have a long way to go to achieve equality. While powerful and successful women have people who admire and support them, there are many more who feel threatened by them. I don't dwell on that, as I learnt a long time ago to brush off criticism and gossip and not take it too personally. Very few arrows pierce my armour today, although it would be wrong to say none do. Just recently someone I started working with informed me that she had been told that I do not work well with women. Fortunately, she made up her own mind within three minutes of meeting me.

I hope that what you get out of this book, apart from some understanding of the financial services industry from an insider's perspective, is a toolkit, or at least the toolkit I would have liked to have had when I was twenty-three. I trust this will make your journey easier and inspire you to fight your battles with the knowledge that, in the end, victory can be yours.

1

A Polish Childhood

MY EARLIEST CHILDHOOD MEMORY IS of walking through a park in autumn, picking fallen chestnuts off the ground, my nanny holding my hand. There is nothing that compares with the smell and crackling sound of newly fallen autumn leaves, golden and red. There is a crispness to that smell that to this day I look out for whenever I am in the northern hemisphere in autumn. And when I find it, I can't resist looking for chestnuts. Another early memory is walking home through the snow in darkness, peering through apartment windows at the Christmas trees inside, snowflakes sparking under the streetlights.

I was born in a town called Gliwice in Poland on 14 October 1969. Dating back to the Renaissance, Gliwice is one of the oldest cities in Upper Silesia, the coal region of southern Poland. Situated close to the German border, the city – called Gleiwitz in German – was annexed by Poland, Austria and Germany at various stages of its turbulent history, finding itself in German hands at the start of the Second World War. It was the site of the infamous Gleiwitz incident, a false-flag attack on the German radio station carried out on the night of 31 August 1939 by German soldiers disguised as Poles, who announced 'Attention! This is Gliwice. The broadcasting station is in Polish hands.' The attack, as intended, was used as justification for the invasion of Poland, which began the following day.

Before the war the city had a mixed population of Poles and Germans. After the war, with Poland's borders shifted west, the city was largely settled by Poles, particularly those displaced from eastern Poland, which had been annexed by the Soviet Union in 1945. Many of these people were academics and professionals from Lwów, my father's parents included. While being transported back to Poland from the Soviet Union on a cattle train in 1947, my grandparents – Waldemar and Helena – decided to get off in Gliwice. By sheer chance, while walking aimlessly down a street, my grandfather carrying a suitcase and my grandmother clutching my father's hand (he was only seven years old at the time), they spotted a plaque attached to the wall of a building and recognised the name printed on it. It was an old friend of my grandfather's from Lwów. With his help, they made Gliwice their home.

As a consequence of that decision, I grew up in communist Poland. Ostensibly ruled by the communist Polish United Workers' Party as a semi-independent satellite state in the Eastern Bloc, true power rested with the Soviet Union, which had installed the government after World War II. On many levels it was a simple political system: the ruling party, allied with the Soviets, exercised complete control over all aspects of one's life, including freedom of movement, while swamping the country with pro-communist and pro-Soviet propaganda. In exchange, they guaranteed everyone free healthcare and education, and full employment. No one had very much, but most people had the same. It was a bit like George Orwell's *Animal Farm*: the only people who had more than others – including houses, cars, access to 'Western' products and ultimately power – were members of the communist party. To put it in perspective, there were approximately three million registered members of the party out of a population of thirty-six million.

Our eighty-square-metre apartment was large by common standards. But it had to house my parents, me and my younger sister and brother, Ashka and Wojtek, and my grandmother who took care of us. The only reason we even qualified for an apartment was because my parents agreed to move from Gliwice to a newly built mining town in Upper Silesia called Jastrzębie-Zdrój. We also qualified for a telephone and a small car, a Fiat 126 nicknamed Maluch, meaning 'the little one'. By today's standards, it looks like a toy. The apartment and the car were luxuries not easily accessible to young people, who tended to live with their parents until they were allocated an apartment of their own. And telephones were just not regarded as a priority by the communists. My parents, both medical doctors, worked six days a week, and we went to school for the same six days. Saturday was not a 'rest day' under communism, even though a lot of people went to work with nothing to do. The closest I have come to reliving that life was watching the 2019 TV series *Chernobyl*. The apartment blocks were a precise match for the estates on which we lived.

My childhood involved a lot of talk about medicine, as every day my parents tried to outdo each other recounting their most terrible cases. I taught myself anatomy by secretly borrowing my mother's medical books. As she was a dermatologist, my early exposure to the human body was less than perfect.

My favourite toys were Lego blocks. To this day I don't know how they made their way to Poland, but there they were, a collection of multicoloured bricks that enabled us to build imaginary cities and inhabit the lives of others. In those days, playing with Lego required a lot of creativity as there were no preconstructed model designs as there are today. There were just blocks of different shapes, colours and sizes. Of everything we left behind, my Lego 'city' was the thing I missed most.

However simple, these were happy years. I had friends and did well at school. Everyone was equal, everyone had the same things and celebrated the same holidays. The uniformity was comforting. There truly was very little diversity, with only one dominant religion, Roman Catholicism. Even today, Poland is regarded as one of the most religiously homogeneous countries in the world. The Roman Catholic Church became the dominant religion as far back as the tenth century and has played a key religious, cultural and political role in the country. The latter is important. Whereas in other Soviet satellites, churches were subject to oppression, in Poland the more progressive members of the communist party, probably recognising the power it held over the average person, formed an informal truce with the church. There would be no persecution provided the church agreed to stay out of politics and recognise the legitimacy of communist rule. As much as religion was not taught at school, we were all frog-marched to weekly religious lessons at the nearby church. Sunday mass was always a crowded affair, with standing room only, and I often felt I would faint. The few children of party members who did not go to church on Sunday were generally ostracised by the rest of the class. My father never went with us to mass, though. Apparently, his senior position in the hospital meant that church attendance would be frowned upon by the authorities. There was another reason too, but I only learnt about it later.

We had no money for fancy holidays or clothes. Things I now take for granted – such as stockings, jeans, perfume and wine – were imported from the West and available only in the specialist Pewex stores (short for Przedsiębiorstwo Eksportu Wewnętrznego – Import Export Company) to politicians, and only then if you had access to US dollars, which most people did not, as it was forbidden to hold foreign currency in cash. As stockings were a precious commodity that could not be easily replaced, most women regularly had them mended by a stockings ladder mender, which was a popular profession. Nevertheless, I remember a lot of cele-bratory holidays and presents. There were women's days, birthdays, name days, parades, Father Christmas in early December, the Christmas angel on Christmas Eve, and the Easter bunny who brought actual presents during the night, together with a bunch of gold-painted twigs tied together like a small broom to remind you to be good. Anything to keep things jovial. In fact, the May Day parade to mark International Workers' Day was so important that attendance was mandatory.

I was a Girl Scout, and I proudly wore my grey uniform and red hand-kerchief around my neck and marched in all the May Day parades. In those days, the Polish Scouting and Guiding Association was one of the very few organisations that retained some level of independence from the ruling party and was incredibly popular, particularly among school-children. I have vivid memories of camping in the forest, running through obstacle courses, which I hated, and taking part in orientation challenges, which I loved.

The air quality in the coal-mining region of Poland was so poor that parents did what they could to get their children out of the cities. Our parents sent us to stay in the countryside over the summer. We rolled in hay, burrowed in haystacks and hitched rides on wagons transporting crops. Summer holidays also involved camping in the northern part of the country, which in those days had pristine lakes and forests. We spent our time picking wild blueberries, strawberries and mushrooms. I regard myself as a bit of an expert at mushroom picking; I'm able to spot one even if it is well covered by pine needles. When my family moved to South Africa, we continued the hobby in the pine forests around Cape Town. This eventually developed into a competition between the local Polish and Italian communities.

When my siblings and I were a bit older, our parents bought a small parcel of land from a farmer in the countryside and constructed a tiny, two-roomed wooden house on the plot. We went there over weekends and during the summer with my grandmother, and she put us to work. We had to dig the vegetable garden with hoes, pick beans and tomatoes, and plant flowers. We also had to collect manure from a farmer across the road to fertilise the garden. Cringing, my sister and I carried it between us in a metal bucket. But we also built bonfires, baking potatoes wrapped in silver foil on the coals and grilling sausages on wooden sticks over the flames.

In winter we went skiing. We were lucky as my parents worked in a hospital largely dedicated to coal miners in the region. Coal miners were revered. Consequently, we had access to coal miners' retreats, large hostel-like buildings in the mountains with complex mazes of rooms. We had the run of the place each winter, and the opportunity to learn how to ski.

I remember having my hair washed with beer. Shampoo was in short supply, but beer was both plentiful and cheap. My mother would bend us over the bathtub and pour a bottle of beer over our hair, then rinse it off with water. To this day I associate the smell of beer with shampoo, and as I don't make a habit of drinking shampoo, I don't drink beer either. While most people associate Poland with vodka, beer was more popular and readily available.

My earliest memories of cooking are a bit too 'authentic' for comfort. No Christmas Eve dinner in Poland was complete without the traditional dish of carp. My parents would buy a live carp a few days before and keep it in the bathtub. At bath time, the writhing carp would have to be temporarily relocated to a plastic bucket in the tiny bathroom. At Easter, it was home-made rabbit pâté. As rabbits were in short supply, we bred our own at our country house. But when Easter came, no one wanted to kill the bunnies, who by that stage all had names. Fortunately, our neighbours were in the same predicament and so the rabbits were promptly swapped between families. My grandmother also bred chickens in the corner of the plot. I don't recall collecting any eggs, but I do remember how to humanely kill a chicken.

My father inherited a small sum of money from a distant great uncle and spent it on a series of sports cars imported from the West. He had a green Ford Capri 2000GT, a silver BMW 3.0 CLS and an orange Renault 17TS. They were among a handful of sports cars in the country. Unfortunately, as fast as he bought them, he crashed them. I was in the car when he wrapped the Ford Capri around a lamp post, and got a bump on my head. With the Renault he was involved in a fifteen-car pile-up. And with a Fiat 125, he crashed because there wasn't a stop sign at an intersection. The Fiat was a standard car used in Poland: you had the 'big Fiat' 125 and the 'small Fiat' 126. In the end we were down to the small Fiat. Later on, in the 1980s, sports cars would have been impractical in any case, as every driver was given a yearly allocation of petrol they could buy. Once exhausted, their cars could not be used unless they bought petrol on the black market.

In reflecting on those years, I must honour three of the powerful women who raised me. The first is my paternal grandmother, Helena, who played an important role in shaping who I am today. In latter-day Poland, she managed a large team of seamstresses, cooked and baked, and taught me how to knit, embroider and crochet, which were considered focused and disciplined activities for a child. She always told me that I could be the best at whatever I did. It was a doctrine she embedded in me as a small child. The memory of her courage, sheer determination to survive and personal strength remains with me today. She and my aunt were the only reason I visited Poland after the fall of communism. My last visit was just before her death in 2016. She died peacefully in her sleep. I am glad I had the opportunity to say goodbye.

The second person is my maternal grandmother, Gienia, who lived with us from the time we moved from Gliwice to Jastrzębie-Zdrój, leaving our nanny behind. With my mother working full-time, she took care of us, the cooking, the cleaning and the washing. She taught us to garden and was merciless in ensuring we did our chores. She never complained. She would later travel with us to South Africa, where she refused to allow us to employ anyone to help her. She continued to cook and clean, as well as indulge in her great passion, tending to our small garden in Kenilworth in Cape Town, until she died of a sudden heart attack. She showed me what hard work looks like.

The third is my nanny, whom I called 'Baba'. She was a gentle woman who loved me like the daughter she never had. She was there, from the beginning, in Gliwice. She taught me how to tie my shoelaces, took me to nursery school and helped me with my homework. My biggest regret was not being able to say goodbye to her when we left. She passed away before I had the opportunity to go back to Poland.

Another woman who loomed large in my life then and again in South Africa where she visited us several times was my parents' stockings ladder mender friend, whom we called 'the pierogi lady'. Pierogi are Polish filled dumplings closely resembling ravioli. She was a true entrepreneur in communist Poland at a time when entrepreneurship was banned. Apart from mending stockings, she frequently travelled to Western Europe and brought back small luxuries, from perfume and chocolate to make-up and stockings, usually by bribing the border guards, but sometimes by smuggling them in her not-insignificantly-proportioned brassier. She sold all these goods on the black market for US dollars, which enabled her to shop at Pewex. In addition, she had great contacts with farmers and could always be relied on for a ham. She eventually opened the best pierogi restaurant in Poland. When she visited us in South Africa, we ate pierogi every day. I always admired her tenacity.

Even though Poland used Western loans to prop up its economy in the 1970s, in exchange for promises of social and economic reforms that never materialised, state propaganda portrayed the capitalist West as the antagonist to the Soviet Union. Censorship and travel restrictions ensured that no one knew any better. Television, like most things, was state-owned and proved to be a useful tool for distributing false information. Only certain, mostly fictional Western movies were allowed, such as *Planet of the Apes* (my favourite at that time). No films that showed how people actually lived in the West – their cars, houses and freedoms – were permitted. Interestingly, Western music, and rock in particular, was judged harmless. This enabled the great rock stars of the era, such as Elton John, Queen, the Rolling Stones, David Bowie, Bruce Springsteen, Billy Joel and Ozzy Osbourne, to perform behind the Iron Curtain. In general, though, the lack of international content led to the development of vibrant local television, magazine and theatre industries in Poland, which continue to this day. Despite continued attempts to improve the image of the Soviet Union, and despite Russian being a compulsory second language at school, general dislike of the Russians was pervasive, albeit only in whispers.

There was a lot of revisionist history taught at school. The fact that Poland was invaded by both Nazi Germany and the Soviet Union in September 1939 as a result of the Molotov–Ribbentrop non-aggression pact signed the month before, in which the two nations agreed on how to divide Poland between them post-invasion, was never mentioned. In the context of World War II, only the Germans were portrayed as aggressors. There was no mention of the Katyn massacre. We had heard about 'Katyn' as children, but did not know what it was; I only found out years later that it was a series of mass executions of nearly 22 000 Polish military officers carried out by the Soviet Union in early 1940. Their bodies were buried in the Katyn forest near Smolensk in western Russia. The Germans stumbled on the mass graves in 1943 and were immediately blamed for the deaths by Joseph Stalin. Russia denied responsibility for the massacre until 2010.

Notwithstanding the gaping holes in the history curriculum, communism did provide me with an incredible education, placing, as it did, particular importance on science, geography and mathematics. When I came to South Africa, I was leaps ahead of my peers in these subjects. This served me well when adjusting to a new life.

The benevolent oppression of the masses can only ever be temporary, however. The main reason is money. These systems invariably go bankrupt, resulting in economic hardship, particularly if the country has no natural resources to sell. In the case of Poland, all its natural resources, primarily coal and steel, were shipped off to the Soviet Union, mostly in exchange for 'industrial cooperation' and little else. By the mid-1970s, lack of economic growth, ageing infrastructure and government subsidies that hid inefficient production were masked by mass employment and artificially high wages. Food distribution had to be managed to ensure sufficient supplies. Although the basics were always there, luxuries such as ham and oranges only became available once a year, at Christmas time. For me, as a child with no understanding of economics, this merely made Christmas more special.

Despite Western loans, the economy was heading for the abyss. What could have been a turning point came about in 1978, two days after my ninth birthday.

On 16 October, Karol Józef Wojtyła, bishop of the ancient Polish city of Kraków, was unexpectedly elected pope. Renamed John Paul II, he was the first non-Italian pope since the sixteenth century and the first Polish pope. He visited Poland a year later and received a raucous welcome in every city. His voice, calling for respect of national and religious traditions, as well as individual freedoms and human rights, was magnified by megaphones and reached every corner of the predominantly Catholic country. Not even the ruling communist party dared censor his message. He gave Poles hope for a better future. But it was not to be, at least not in the short term.

While the economy had surface cracks in the 1970s, the 1980s brought real fissures. The first that I remember came in June 1980 when the government proclaimed the need to ration the allocation of meat. Up until then, rationing had occurred without any official pronouncement. The sixty per cent price increase that followed, unaffordable to most even when meat was available, sparked strikes in factories across Poland, from the northern coastal towns to the southern coal-mining region. By mid-July there were over fifty active strikes across the country. In hindsight, the Polish nation was so tired of oppression that anything could have ignited unrest. I recall becoming politically aware for the first time because of the complete disappearance of my favourite food, ham – already a rare treat. I was yet to become a vegetarian.

The tide turned in favour of the striking workers on 14 August 1980, when the Lenin Shipyard in Gdańsk in northern Poland joined the strike. The massive strike of over 17 000 shipyard workers was led by Lech Wałęsa, an electrician and former employee who had been dismissed for illegal union activities. Their twenty-one demands, which included the legalisation of independent trade unions, the right to strike, the release of political prisoners and increased freedom of expression, were written on an aged white board, now on display at the European Solidarity Centre in Gdańsk. The shipyard was sealed off, but several people slipped through the roadblocks to spread the news. Despite heavy censorship of the press at the time, I recall seeing images of the striking workers, who were described by the regime as leading some form of insurrection.

Within days, the strikes became more organised and collaborative, with committees forming in the various regions. In an unexpected twist, the lower ranks of the ruling party, including security forces, joined the striking workers. This eventually brought the government to the negotiating table, and on 31 August, the Gdańsk Agreement was signed, allowing the formation of trade unions independent of party control and agreeing to wage increases and limits on censorship. A month later, the decentralised factory-level 'trade union committees' converted into branches of Solidarity, the first independent trade union in the Eastern Bloc, representing nearly ninety per cent of all workers in Poland. Over the next year, Solidarity expanded to a membership of ten million, almost a quarter of the Polish population, and morphed into a national reform movement. Unfortunately, this did nothing to improve economic conditions in Poland and it did not last long.

As the economy spiralled downwards, foodstuffs and basic household items, including meat, coffee, sugar, laundry detergent and cigarettes, started disappearing from the shop shelves. In December 1980, my parents were issued with green ration cards, which allowed them to buy two kilograms of meat and one packet of butter a week. A postage-stamp-like coupon on a ration card was not a guarantee, however; it was merely a ticket to the game. Desperate people started forming queues at shops the night before in the hope that something, anything, would be delivered in the morning. Some people made a good living by standing in queues on behalf of others. Apparently in Hungary there was a running joke: 'Do you know what a Polish sandwich looks like? Two slices of bread and a ration card for the meat in between.'

Those with families in the countryside fared better as they had access to farm-grown products. We didn't have anyone, apart from the pierogi lady, who helped out where she could. A few chickens and a couple of rabbits were not a substitute for daily bread. Bizarrely, the only things on the shelves of our local store were bottles and bottles of vinegar. I remember them distinctly because, while on an errand to check the length of the queue, I knocked some over and they broke, leaving me traumatised. I had to use the little money I had to pay for the vinegar.

As the crisis deepened, hunger demonstrations by mostly women and their children took place in cities and towns across the country, peaking in August 1981. The situation was not exclusive to Poland, however. As conditions worsened, over three million people across the Soviet satellite states made the decision to escape to the West in search of a better life. My family were among them.

2

Escape from Poland

UNDER COMMUNISM, FREEDOM OF MOVEMENT was not a right and was tightly controlled. You were only allowed to leave the country if you had a temporary pass stamped with both your departure and return dates. You also had to leave a 'hostage' behind, at least one close family member, to ensure that you would return. My parents hatched a plan. Leaving my brother and grandmother behind, they took my sister and me on 'holiday' to Italy. It was the first time I had left the Eastern Bloc. We had little money, travelled in our tiny Fiat and camped outside all the ancient cities. Our daily treat was yoghurt. While ice cream was plentiful, yoghurt was unknown in Poland. I know I should have admired the grand sites more, like the Sistine Chapel in Vatican City and the Uffizi Gallery in Florence, but my overwhelming desire was to own a Japanese Monchhichi doll, a small fuzzy stuffed monkey that was advertised on huge banners along the highways. I do have a photograph of me and my sister standing in St Mark's Square outside the Basilica di San Marco in Venice. Venice remains my favourite city in the world, and I have been back many times. I always return to the precise spot where that photo was taken. It puts how short life is into perspective.

We returned to Poland a few days earlier than our travel passes indicated. In the meantime, my grandmother had applied for passes for herself and my brother which overlapped with our return. In the days before computers, there were no centralised records, so the authorities had no way of telling that the dates of our passes overlapped. A couple of days after our return from Italy, with no warning or explanation, my parents announced that we were going on yet another trip. We could each pack a small suitcase. There was tension in the air. My uncle came over and the adults whispered in the corner. Although no one told us what was going on, we somehow knew we would not be coming back. Perhaps the fact that my mother hung all the gold chains she owned around our necks gave us a hint. I packed my little suitcase with my nicest clothes, nothing else. My last memory of our apartment is a snapshot of my Lego city, carefully constructed on a sideboard in my bedroom.

We left the apartment after dark. I had a premonition that it may be a long time before I returned to Poland. It was 31 August 1981 and I was eleven years old. I stooped down, picked up a handful of soil and put it in the pocket of my favourite red coat. I don't know what happened to that soil, or my coat, but it was a symbolic gesture rather than a material one.

We split up. My mother, sister and I took a train to Vienna, while my father, brother and grandmother crossed the border by car. The plan was to meet at McDonald's in the centre of Vienna the next morning. From Vienna, we would rely on welfare organisations to help us get to the United States, a plan I only learnt about much later. But it didn't work out that way. We ended up in a refugee camp outside Vienna instead. Located in the small town of Traiskirchen, the camp was situated on an old military base. To this day, it remains one of the largest refugee processing centres in the European Union. As recently as 2015, human rights group Amnesty International criticised the conditions in the camp as 'inhumane'. Guarded by soldiers, we were fingerprinted, issued with a blanket, pillow, set of aluminium dishes, soap, toothbrush and toothpaste, and taken to a large room with metal bunk beds. Some of the scenes from that camp still haunt me. The man who slept in the bunk above me moaned through the night. He had walked all the way from Ukraine and had gangrene. The toilets were flooded. We were not allowed to leave. Everywhere scared and stressed people sat around waiting. Their powerlessness was palpable.

My parents soon learnt that they were waiting for an 'interview' to explain why we sought asylum. If your reasons were not good enough, you had to stay in the camp indefinitely. If you were accepted as a potential refugee, you would be rehoused while you applied for immigration to a sponsor country. We were luckier than most. Because we were a family unit and my parents' explanations clearly made some sense, after a while we were relocated to a 'guesthouse' in the rural village of Bad Kreuzen in Upper Austria. There was a large refugee camp in town, but it was full. Once in the guesthouse, there was nothing to do but wait to be accepted as official immigrants to the United States, Australia, Canada, New Zealand or Germany, among others. I recently read a *New York Times* article from that time describing how all these countries increased their official annual immigration quotas to accommodate refugees from Eastern Europe.

Living in a village in the Austrian countryside may sound idyllic, but it was nothing of the sort. We had no money, we did not speak German, the Austrian children threw stones at us and called us names, and my father dug ditches for a meagre wage. The future was unknown. The most exciting event was burrowing through piles of used clothing donated to the Caritas Catholic relief organisation. The guesthouse owner fed us the bare minimum. On Fridays, we were served a mystery ball – basically all the scraps of the week rolled into a giant ball of dough and boiled. No one ate on Fridays. Life seemed to be suspended. Cut off from family and friends, we waited. Our time was spent doing a massive puzzle of Pope John Paul II presiding over St Peter's Basilica. We played with the other refugee children in the corridors. One girl had a Barbie doll and was the envy of everyone. Our happiest moment came at Christmas. With what little money he had earned, my father bought me and my sister the Japanese Monchhichi dolls we so coveted. They came in four colours. Mine was black and I have it to this day.

The guesthouse was never inspected by the Austrian authorities. The government 'hosted' us because they were obliged to do so in terms of the Geneva Convention, which sets out the rights of refugees who are granted asylum and the responsibilities of nations towards them. As the upkeep of the refugees was paid for by the sponsor countries, the Austrian government and the United Nations, housing refugees became a profitable business for Austrian guesthouse owners.

In October 1981, a little over a month after we fled Poland, General Wojciech Jaruzelski became a Soviet-controlled puppet prime minister. Similar to what happened in South Africa in 1985, he reversed course on what seemed to be an initial willingness to introduce reforms to release Poland from the shackles of the communist system and relax the Soviet Union's grasp on the country. On 13 December 1981, he declared martial law and banned Solidarity. This was a function of the trade union's increasing demands on the one hand and pressure from the Soviet Union on the other. Perversely, this worked in our favour. Overnight, the status of all Poles trapped in refugee camps in Austria changed from 'economic refugee' to 'political refugee'. This was useful in negotiating where we went next.

One day in March 1982, my parents overheard that the South African Defence Force and a number of coal-mining companies were recruiting medical doctors, architects, engineers and even musicians and cooks to work in South Africa. I guess the South African government and industrial sector realised that in the refugee camps they had access to cheap, skilled labour. My parents lodged their CVs on an off-chance, and were called to an interview in the South African embassy in Vienna, where a man dressed in a military uniform asked one question over and over again: 'Were you members of the Communist Party?' A couple of weeks later, we were on a South African Airways flight to Johannesburg. It was the first time I had been on an aeroplane. All I remember is that I mistakenly tried to open the main door of the cabin in search of a toilet. Thankfully, an alert stewardess managed to stop me from fiddling with the lock.

I often wonder what life I would have lived if I had remained in Poland.

As fate would have it, while I was writing this book, I was invited to visit Poland for the most extended period since my childhood. I went to art galleries and museums, visited several towns, and met many interesting people who invited me into their homes. I saw amazing art collections, ate at great restaurants, and joined in the jovial singing after a few too many bottles of wine.

The trip was also a fascinating journey into the past and provided some context to my childhood memories. It also gave me some insight into what it might have been like if I'd spent my teenage years in Poland. At the time, all I could do was observe from a distance. It struck me that the fall of Soviet-style communism in Poland bears an uncanny similarity to events that played out in the dying days of apartheid in South Africa almost five years later.

While in Poland, aside from current politicians, I was privileged to meet Lech Wałęsa, the co-founder and former leader of Solidarity, and Polish prime minister after the fall of the Berlin Wall. Wałęsa is in his seventies now, but as energetic as he was in the 1980s. He gave me a signed photograph of himself being carried on the shoulders of his supporters in the Lenin Shipyard during that fateful strike. He had a simple, albeit not unique, message to convey. In his view, the most serious problems facing the world today are climate change and the pace at which technological advancement is destroying jobs. If the world's leaders do not unite in a global debate to address these issues, the future looks bleak. I think a lot of countries have recognised this, but many have yet to come to the table, including South Africa with its coal-based power generation.

Events in Poland in the 1980s, although removed from South Africa, cast a shadow over our daily lives as we still had family there who needed our support. The fact that the ruling communist party in Poland, after initially negotiating with Solidarity, reneged on the Gdańsk Agreement was a reminder of the reluctance of regimes around the world to let go of power, however legitimate or illegitimate that power might be. Not dissimilarly, after apparently considering significant political reforms, President P.W. Botha did a turnaround and delivered his infamous Rubicon speech on 15 August 1985. I remember the anticipation before the speech, as the world expected him to announce the abolition of apartheid, but instead he announced to the world that he was not willing to end apartheid and that he would not release Nelson Mandela from prison. 'I believe we are today crossing the Rubicon ... there can be no turning back,' he declared. Economic sanctions followed, South Africa was shunned by the world's political and business communities, and the rest is history. It was no Rubicon.

After the Polish government introduced martial law and banned Solidarity in 1981, its leaders, including Wałęsa, were arrested. Censorship expanded and soldiers appeared on the streets. On my return visit to Poland, I asked someone who had lived next door to us what martial law looked like in Jastrzębie-Zdrój. She told me that she woke up one morning to deep snow, military personnel patrolling the streets and tanks blocking every major road in the city. From her balcony, next door to our old apartment, she saw a man walking towards the tanks carrying the Polish flag. He fell down, and she realised that he had been shot. I watched a video at the Solidarity museum in Gdańsk of General Jaruzelski delivering the news of the military takeover on national television and justifying the deployment of the army. Today it looks almost comical. In 1981, it was terrifying.

Similar to events in South Africa four years later, the introduction of martial law led to many countries imposing economic sanctions on Poland. Whatever the good intention, this only intensified the economic hardship of Poland's citizens. On our arrival in South Africa, my father started sending food parcels to his family trapped back home, as did many other emigrants. The food parcels included everything from coffee to rice – anything non-perishable. Incredibly, they all reached their destination. A friend told me that many families survived living from parcel to parcel. The foodstuffs also became valuable currency and could be swapped for other goods.

Martial law was lifted after eighteen months, but many of its controls, as well as food rationing, remained in place throughout the 1980s. So did our parcels. Solidarity moved underground, just as the ANC had done in South Africa.

In October 1983, Wałęsa was awarded the Nobel Peace Prize. It was collected by his wife, as he feared that if he left Poland, he would not be allowed to return.

Communism ultimately collapsed under the weight of the economic and political sanctions, and the fact that the Soviet Union had simply run out of money. Once again, the situation was not dissimilar to that of apartheid South Africa. Mikhail Gorbachev, the eighth and last leader of the Soviet Union, was forced to adopt political and social reforms, namely *glasnost* (openness) and *perestroika* (restructuring). He also cut off financial support to the satellite states, including Poland. This led to the eventual decline of Soviet domination across the region. In February 1989, crippled by debt, high inflation, inefficient state-owned enterprises, food shortages and negligible exports, the communist government declared their willingness to negotiate with Wałęsa and Solidarity once again. A new chapter had begun, not only for Poland, but for the whole of Eastern Europe.

In August 1989, Wałęsa was instrumental in the formation of a non-communist coalition government – the first in the Eastern Bloc. A year later, in December 1990, he ran as an independent and became the first non-communist president of Poland in forty-five years. All of this only four or five years before Nelson Mandela created a government of national unity in South Africa. Both leaders supported a peaceful transition of power. Solidarity acted as an inspiration for other anti-communist uprisings in Eastern Europe, which ultimately saw the collapse of the Soviet Union in 1991. The most potent symbol from this time was the fall of the Berlin Wall on 9 November 1989. It is a moment I will always remember – people climbing over the wall and reuniting with family, friends and complete strangers on the other side. Many years later, I visited Berlin and bought a piece of the 'wall', although rumour has it that the Berlin Wall has been sold several times over.

Like the ANC in South Africa, Solidarity had to transition from an anti-government movement to a governing political party, a role for which it was ill-prepared. It soon began to lose popularity, and by 1993 its relevance had waned. The same scenario is slowly playing out in South Africa, where the ANC is barely clinging to a majority vote.

While I do draw parallels between Wałęsa and Mandela, and Solidarity and the ANC, nothing can compare to the horror of apartheid or the twenty-seven years that Mandela spent on Robben Island. It is the trajectory of the decline of the unsustainable regimes against which they fought that is eerily similar. As an avid follower of global politics and economics and how the two intersect, I always keep in mind the words of Spanish philosopher George Santayana: 'Those who cannot remember the past are condemned to repeat it.' Every time I hear it, the quote sparks a memory of my family's fate, a traumatising story that was hidden from us as children until after we had left Poland.

3

Roots

MY TRUE SURNAME IS NOT WIERZYCKA. Wierzycka is a surname made up by my father's parents after the Second World War to hide the fact that they were Jewish, because being openly Jewish remained dangerous in Poland, even after the Nazis had been defeated. If not for that, my name today would be Magda Getreu. Getreu in Hebrew means 'the faithful'. Clinging to the past but in need of a new identity, my grandparents chose Wierzycka, a derivative of a Polish word meaning 'the believer'.

I had no idea about this side of my history until we had already left Poland and were living in South Africa. One day my father called us together to reveal what he regarded as a momentous family secret. He was Jewish, he told us, and his parents had survived the Holocaust. It clearly took a heavy emotional toll on him to finally divulge this. To us, however, it meant little. It was the first time I had heard the word 'Jew' in a context other than the doctrines of the Roman Catholic Church. I didn't understand the meaning of what we were being told until much later. I certainly did not realise its significance to my own life.

Poland has an unfortunate history of anti-Semitism, and it remains a sensitive topic in the current political climate. To understand it, one needs to delve deep into the history of the region, as far back as the Middle Ages, but, more recently, to propaganda disseminated by Polish nationalists before the outbreak of World War II, then by the Nazis during the war and finally by the communists and opportunists after the war. There have been suggestions by scholars that Poland provided fertile ground for Adolf Hitler's campaign of extermination.

To avoid the pogroms after World War II, my grandfather Waldemar hid his family's origins with the help of some very kind Polish people, including a Roman Catholic priest. And it remained hidden, until that day in South Africa when our father told us the truth, a truth that went straight over my head. It was only years later while at university, and then again more recently, that I decided to explore my Jewish ancestry.

My father's mother, Helena, who lived to the age of ninety-four, was an incredibly strong and brave woman. In 2012, a few years before she died, my sister and I went to Poland to record our family's oral history. Family histories are important: they provide perspective and insight and can help us understand who we are and where we come from. Listening to my grandmother certainly helped explain some of the family dynamics we had experienced growing up. Not every difficulty we faced was because we were refugees. There was so much more to my family's history in Poland than I understood at the time.

For some reason, as a child I never wondered why my father's side of the family was almost non-existent. On my mother's side, there was my grandmother and my mother's brother. My grandfather, who was a furniture maker, died when I was very young. There was a lot of talk about family estrangements to explain the limited contact we had with my mother's extended family, but I knew their names, had met some of them and even attended a funeral. On my father's side there were my grandparents and my aunt, but there was never any mention of great-aunts or uncles or cousins, there was just a void. No one ever talked about the past. Much has been written about the lifelong effects of the trauma experienced by survivors of the Holocaust, both on themselves and their children. Like many others, my grandparents suppressed their trauma in order to cope. They buried the memories and focused on rebuilding their lives in post-war Poland. But they lived in constant fear of being 'outed' as Jewish. Looking back, I can clearly remember the inexplicable tension in their apartment when we went to visit. At the time, all I knew about them was that they were from Lwów, which had been annexed by Russia after the war.

It took my grandmother seventy years to tell the story of her family and how she and my grandfather had survived the war. Even when my father was a grown man, she could not bring herself to tell him. I recently learnt from my father that he knows a lot less about his family's history than I do. Perhaps it was easier for my grandmother to pass the story on to a generation once removed. When my sister and I visited her, I got the feeling it was important to her that her family's history finally be spoken aloud and preserved in our memories. I am glad she did it, and I am sorry that my grandfather died without being able to do the same.

My grandmother's family was prosperous. Her grandfather was the biggest supplier of horses to the Austrian army at the turn of the century. Consequently, prior to the war, her parents owned a lot of land and property. They lived affluently in Lwów. My grandmother went to an exclusive school for young ladies and learnt French and Russian. My grandfather studied medicine at the university in Lwów, where he qualified in 1938. My grandmother told us how hard he and the other Jewish students found it. There were strict limits on how many Jews could be accepted to study. In 1935, the university adopted a policy of enforced segregation, whereby Jewish students were required to sit or stand in separate sections in classrooms and lecture halls, known as 'ghetto benches'. The official policy was only in place a few months before it was overturned due to criticism from both home and abroad, but it was an important signifier of the latent anti-Semitism that had been brewing in Poland since the turn of the century.

In September 1939, Lwów was captured and occupied by the Soviet Union in terms of the Molotov–Ribbentrop Pact between the Nazis and the Soviets. Then, in June 1941, it was taken over by the Germans as part of Operation Barbarossa, whereby Germany declared war on the Soviet Union. When the Nazis took control, my father's entire family was herded into the Lwów Ghetto. While Jewish ghettos were set up immediately on the invasion of Poland, mass extermination camps were only established in 1942 after the infamous Wannsee Conference, where the 'final solution' to the Jewish problem was agreed on. It began with random raids on Jewish apartments to forcibly remove people under the guise of 'resettlement' to unrevealed locations. My grandmother lived through one such raid. Fortunately, on seeing an infant – my father – in her arms, the Germans left them alone for a time. After this, my grandmother's father organised fake Ukrainian papers for her, which enabled her and my father to live outside the ghetto. She was a talented seamstress and found work making uniforms for the German soldiers.

Because there was no Polish army, my grandfather voluntarily joined the Russian army as a medical doctor, as he wanted to fight the Germans with 'a gun in his hand'. Soon thereafter he was captured and imprisoned in a slave-labour camp in Darnica near Kiev. He proved equally useful to the Germans, and was put to work as a doctor. He was sufficiently trusted to be allowed to travel to Lwów by military train on a special pass to bring typhus medication back to the camp, as the Germans were petrified of typhus. No one suspected he was Jewish. As life in Lwów became more dangerous for Jews in hiding, my grandmother persuaded him to move her and my father closer to the camp. My grandfather was reluctant as the journey would endanger all their lives. He eventually 'smuggled' them out separately, my father on a train full of German soldiers on their way to the Eastern Front who fed him chocolates. He developed diarrhoea and, for obvious reasons, my grandfather could not change his nappy in front of the soldiers.

As the Soviets advanced on Kiev in late 1943, my grandfather's German supervisor warned him of the Nazis' intent to burn down the camp the next day and either take all its prisoners with them or kill them. My grandmother had one day to come up with a plan to save her husband and herself. Faced with being taken forcibly by the Germans, she told them she had typhus. As for my grandfather, she smuggled him out of the camp dressed as a woman. As they walked along the road, a German soldier stopped them, having seen through the disguise. My grandmother offered him her only valuable, a ring on her finger. He refused to take the ring and instead asked for the scarf around her neck for his girlfriend. They survived through the humanity of one man. And I have the ring today.

My grandparents never knew what became of their families, other than my grandmother's father, who was apparently shot in the street when he did not bow down low enough to a passing German soldier. The Lwów Ghetto was liquidated in June 1943. All surviving inhabitants were deported to either the Bełżec extermination camp or the Janowska concentration camp. Mothers, fathers, sisters, brothers, aunts, uncles, cousins: they all simply disappeared from the face of the earth, remaining only in memories and photographs. It is likely they all died in Janowska. Established on the outskirts of Lwów, this was where the Germans conducted torture and executions to music. Imprisoned musicians, including members of the Lwów National Opera, were forced to play the same tune, 'Tango of Death', over and over again. On the eve of the camp's liberation by the Russians, the Nazis executed the entire orchestra.

I later learnt that, of my grandmother's family in Lwów, only an uncle survived. He was imprisoned at Auschwitz and, after its liberation, moved to Paris where he opened a large legal practice specialising in fighting for reparations for Jews who lost their property in the post-war border reallocation. It was he who left us the inheritance my father squandered on sports cars.

Of my grandfather's family, there were no known survivors.

Because this book will be read by my sons, I want to record the names of their Jewish ancestors. My grandmother's name was Helena Romana Bank, daughter of Arnold Herman and Fani Bank. My grandfather's name was Waldemar Emanuel Gustaw Getreu, son of Julian and Helena Getreu. The POLIN Museum of the History of Polish Jews, on the site of the former Warsaw Ghetto, offers to rebuild your family tree based on the extensive records in their possession. We have decided to find out more.

Lwów was annexed by the Soviet Union after the Yalta Conference of February 1945, a shameful meeting where the chief Allied leaders – Joseph Stalin, Franklin D. Roosevelt and Winston Churchill – discussed and ratified the post-war reorganisation of Germany and Europe, and the Polish borders in particular.

When the war ended, and it was time to go 'home', none of the surviving Jews had papers to prove their identity. The Russians, now occupying regions that before the war had belonged to Poland, relied on people's ability to speak Polish, including pronunciation and accent, to determine whether they could settle in the newly designated Poland. My grandfather had no trouble establishing that he was Polish and was eventually permitted to leave for Poland, despite the Russians finding his medical skills too useful to let him go easily. My grandmother, however, was a talented linguist and fluent in four languages, having added German to her Russian, Polish and French during the war. She was told that, given her pitch-perfect St Petersburg accent, she was clearly Russian and had to stay. She eventually successfully pleaded her and my grandfather's case to the political commissar who ran the Ukrainian territories at the time, Nikita Khrushchev. Khrushchev went on to replace Joseph Stalin as the First Secretary of the Communist Party of the Soviet Union, a post he occupied from 1953 to 1964.

My father told me that he and my grandparents visited Lwów only once after the war. When they reached the house in which my grandfather grew up, he refused to get out of the car. No one spoke. They drove on. Such was their trauma.

But the Holocaust was not the only horror to befall Poland's Jews.

On 4 July 1946, in the Polish city of Kielce, forty-two Jews were killed and over forty wounded in a bloody pogrom perpetrated by Polish soldiers, police officers and civilians. The killings were ignited by a rumour that the Jews were kidnapping Christian children for ritual sacrifice. This event precipitated a mass exodus of Polish Jewry from the country.

Two decades later, in September 1967, the ruling communist Polish United Workers' Party embarked on a campaign to purge Jews from all senior positions in the military and government. This was triggered by the Six-Day War in June 1967, an armed conflict between Israel and an Arab coalition including Egypt, Jordan and Syria and backed by the Eastern Bloc. Poland and the Soviet Union severed all diplomatic ties with Israel. Jews, particularly those sympathetic to Israel, were denounced as enemies of the state. By 1968, a virulent anti-Semitic campaign led by the state-controlled media had taken hold. Described variously as a 'linguistic' or 'symbolic' pogrom, discriminatory measures were used to remove Jews from important positions in all areas of Polish society. They were consequently dismissed from all civil-service posts, expelled from the Polish United Workers' Party, removed from teaching positions in schools and universities, and pressurised to leave the country. Those who agreed to go – over 14 000 of them – were immediately stripped of their Polish citizenship. They were nobodies who belonged nowhere. While there were protests against these measures, particularly among university students and intellectuals, and while many Polish people stood up for their neighbours, it was not enough. Vilified and socially isolated, most Jews left Poland never to return. Some of the most skilled ended up in Canada, the United States, Australia, South Africa and, of course, Israel.

Restrictions were placed on what they could take with them. No official documentation, including birth certificates and university degrees, could be taken. This effectively stripped Jewish emigrants of their dignity and identity, as well as their ability to seek employment in their fields of expertise. Nothing produced before 1945 was permitted, including family photographs. This was particularly brutal given that, after the Holocaust, photographs were often all that remained of loved ones. Our own emigration, over a decade later, looked very similar. We took no documentation with us. It was only months later that my grandmother smuggled out our birth certificates and my parents' university diplomas.

My parents told me that their suitcases were packed and ready to leave in 1968. The only thing that stopped them was that my grandfather's superior, a Pole, intervened with the authorities on his behalf. As much as they hid their Jewish identity from their neighbours, my grandfather's medical diploma bore his real name. Having lived through the Holocaust, he refused to leave Poland. He was a doctor of great standing by that stage, and retaining his job meant he could stay. For the second time in his life, he was saved by the person for whom he worked.

My trip to Poland to revisit the darker side of my family's history was enlightening in so many ways. On a visit to the POLIN Museum in

Warsaw, I heard the following statistics: Before World War II, roughly 3.3 million Jews lived in Poland, more than in any other country in Europe. Approximately 350 000 survived the Holocaust, my grandparents and father included. They did so by hiding in the Soviet Union in forests, in ditches on farms, under floorboards, in cupboards, often sheltered by families at great personal risk. Many, like my grandparents, used their wits. Of the 350 000 survivors, 300 000 left Poland after the war, largely as a result of the Kielce and other pogroms. After the 1968 purge, only about 30 000 remained, including my grandparents and their, by now, two children. What are the chances of me, my brother, my sister and our children being alive today? Negligible at best. Today, according to our guide at the POLIN Museum, there are only 7 500 people who live openly as Jews in Poland, but the number has been steadily increasing since Poland entered the European Union.

I had the privilege on my visit to meet another Polish luminary, Marian Turski, an Auschwitz survivor who became a famous historian, activist and journalist. Like my grandparents, he too changed his name (he was born Mosze Turbowicz). Turski lost thirty-nine family members to the Holocaust. He has always been a libertarian and took part in the 1965 marches from Selma to Montgomery led by Martin Luther King against racial segregation in the American South. He continues to be involved in the Jewish Historical Institute in Poland, the Association of Jewish Combatants and Victims of World War II, and the International Auschwitz Council, among others. He was instrumental in establishing the POLIN Museum. His ninetieth birthday in 2016 was marked by congratulations from many heads of state, including German chancellor Angela Merkel, US president Barack Obama and former Israeli prime minister Shimon Peres.

Turski's wisdom is widely sought after. He delivered a powerful message on 27 January 2020, marking International Holocaust Remembrance Day and the seventy-fifth anniversary of the liberation of Auschwitz. In this divided world, his words have never rung truer. 'Auschwitz did not fall from the sky,' he said. 'It began with small forms of persecution of

Jews. It happened; it means it can happen anywhere. That is why human rights and democratic constitutions must be defended. The eleventh commandment is important: Don't be indifferent. Do not be indifferent when you see historical lies. Do not be indifferent when any minority is discriminated against. Do not be indifferent when power violates a social contract.'

A few months later, in a commemoration speech marking the annual 2 August Holocaust Memorial Day for Sinti and Roma, and referring to the global Covid-19 pandemic that gripped the world at the time, he said: 'We are all full of fear as human beings, but eventually an effective vaccine will be discovered, or another way to prevent the pandemic, just as it has been previously done in many other cases. However, there is another vicious disease that affects Poland and Europe – it is the hatred against another human being, it infects minds and it is difficult to find a cure for it. If we are not able to overcome our resentments towards the others, that is to say, to anti-gypsyism, anti-Semitism, xenophobia, fear of someone else, anxiety, this is much worse than any epidemic, it poisons our minds.' His words are relevant not only to Europe, but to every single country in the world where there is intolerance of other human beings; be it racism, sexism, religious extremism or homophobia, his words will resonate no matter where you live.

When we met, he spoke to me about the importance of the POLIN Museum in that the history of Jews in Poland should not be solely defined by what happened in the twentieth century. Polish Jews and Poles have coexisted peacefully since the twelfth century. The museum is a commemoration of that shared history rather than a Holocaust memorial like Auschwitz-Birkenau.

Nevertheless, Auschwitz has a particular significance to me. It was built as a death camp by the Nazis, and at least 1.1 million people, most of them Jewish, died in its gas chambers or from starvation, cold and disease. As most of my father's family died in concentration camps, I have visited Auschwitz several times and ensured that my children understand their heritage.

Despite the intergenerational trauma suffered by my family in Poland, it would be remiss of me not to mention that I have met some incredible people in current-day Poland. These people are generous to a fault, highly intelligent, knowledgeable about arts, culture and politics, lovers of opera, and not afraid to speak out. They do not represent the past. I do not blame them for what happened and I would never tar every Pole with the same brush. However, it is important to me that the history of Poland's Jews does not die with the survivors. Not many people will visit the POLIN Museum. If I can contribute by reflecting on some of the facts, facts that affected my family, I will have done a good job.

I am often asked about my nationality. On social media, I am accused of not being South African or, at least, not being South African enough. In the United Kingdom, people see my surname and immediately identify me as Polish.

So how *do* I identify? I was born in Poland but raised in South Africa. My father is Jewish, my mother is Polish. At the end of the day, I believe that nationality comes down to a feeling and personal choice. No one has the right to tell me who I am or should be. I am who I choose to be. I find it the most difficult to say that I am Polish as my time there was curtailed by events beyond my control, and I am only now becoming more familiar with the country. I feel I can claim to be South African despite not being born here and despite English being my second language. I grew up here, I work here, my children were born here. South Africa, after all, is a melting pot of all kinds of nationalities, races and religions. But I also claim my Jewish heritage and I refuse to apologise for that. My family died in the Holocaust; they took part in the Warsaw Uprising. The fact that my mother is not Jewish cannot strip me of that identity, irrespective of ancient doctrines that dictate the rules for inclusion.

During my university years, I visited Poland with some Jewish friends. My grandfather was furious. He took me aside and told me that being Jewish had brought him nothing but the utmost misery and pain, and that I should not search for my Jewish roots as he had spent a lifetime trying to forget that those roots ever existed. Listening to him was tragic and moving, his trauma visceral, but it did not and does not stop me.

In the early 2000s, I finally visited Israel. My grandmother made sure I went to Yad Vashem, Israel's official memorial to the victims of the Holocaust, in Jerusalem. She asked me to check if her sister had ever registered her name there, in the hope that perhaps she had survived. Her name was not there, but my grandmother never stopped looking and remembering.

I often think that most people can be divided into three groups. On one side are those who hate, particularly along racial, religious and ethnocentric lines. There is often no rational reason for their hatred. On the other side are those who speak out against the haters. In the middle are the vast majority, who stay neutral. They do not get involved. They do not speak out. They ignore and pretend that they do not see what is happening around them. Another relevant quote comes to mind: 'Evil triumphs when good men do nothing.' This is true of what happened to the Jews in Poland before, during and after the war. It is true of what happened in South Africa during apartheid and then again during Jacob Zuma's presidency. It is true of what ninety-three-year-old Marian Turski said in his 2020 Holocaust Remembrance Day speech, 'Because if you *are* indifferent, you will not even notice it when upon your own heads, and upon the heads of your descendants, another Auschwitz falls from the sky.' You get to choose which camp you belong to. I know the one I have chosen. I do wonder, though, to what extent my choice has been influenced by my heritage.

4

Pretoria Girl

I KNEW NOTHING ABOUT SOUTH AFRICA when we landed in Johannesburg on 8 March 1982. I was only twelve years old, and had travelled from communist Poland, via refugee camps in Austria, and I was now on the other side of the world. It was an utterly unfamiliar place, and all that my parents had was five hundred US dollars in cash. My family was faced with the challenge that all immigrants face: to build a new life in a strange land.

We were picked up from Johannesburg's Jan Smuts Airport by a military van and transported to the unpronounceable Voortrekkerhoogte, an army base in Pretoria where we would stay in temporary accommodation. In those days, Johannesburg and Pretoria seemed far apart, divided by scrubland that was burned in winter to prevent wildfires. We had swapped the rich greenery of Europe for the blackened bush of Africa. I remember staring at the barren landscape through the van's windows, and my amazement at the soil being a reddish colour as opposed to the pitch-black that we were used to.

We were put up in a nursing hostel at first. On arrival, my mother and grandmother sat on the iron beds and cried, while my siblings and I stood around in silence. Everything was a challenge. We spoke no English, and of course no Afrikaans. We knew nothing about South Africa, its politics or its history. We had no money to speak of, and no belongings. We knew no one. The Highveld winter was unlike any winter I'd experienced before. Coming from the northern hemisphere, we were used to four distinct seasons, as opposed to sudden transitions from warmth to cold, and we missed the central heating that kept one snug. I am not sure my parents would have made the decision to come to South Africa if they had known more about it. There was no internet in those days and South Africa was regarded in Poland as a land of gold. There was a small Polish community in Johannesburg and even a Polish church, but living in Pretoria, we were far removed from it.

The biggest challenge we faced was how to build a brand-new life in a foreign country. My parents sacrificed much in leaving Poland, where they were both well-respected medical doctors with double specialisations. They had a better life than most. They were better travelled than most Poles, compliments of the legacy my father inherited from his uncle in Paris. They were certainly a lot better informed about the standard of living and freedoms offered by the West. I have no doubt that they left Poland to give their children a better chance in life. Starting from scratch in their early forties was never going to be easy.

My parents were recruited to work in 1 Military Hospital. Despite being used as specialists by the hospital, they were paid general practitioners' salaries and were restricted to working exclusively for the public sector. They were told that their degrees, being Polish, were not recognised in the private sector. After four months, on 30 June, we moved into a three-bedroom flat in Sunnyside, a lower-middle-class suburb in Pretoria full of apartment buildings. With their meagre wages, my parents had to buy everything, from cutlery and linen to furniture, all while keeping a roof over our heads and food on the table. Somehow, they managed it. My father was a great juggler of credit cards. He opened accounts with every bank that would extend him credit and kept moving money around, robbing Peter to pay Paul.

Our precarious financial position had a surprising consequence. In those days, women in South Africa were second-class citizens. In terms of taxation, working married women were taxed at a much higher rate than single women. This was meant to disincentivise women from working. When my parents learnt of this, and given that every cent mattered, they secretly divorced. They remarried years later, equally secretively, when the tax laws were equalised. My own approach to money has been deeply influenced by my family's early struggles. As much as I am willing to take risks, every risk I take is calculated. I don't start businesses unless I can see the break-even point. My brother and sister are even more conservative than me when it comes to debt and money management.

Things improved around 1994, when a number of black doctors who had qualified in Eastern Europe returned to South Africa demanding that their qualifications be recognised. This was good news for my father, who started looking elsewhere for opportunities to earn a better salary. He bought a series of clinics in the Transkei. The clinics amounted to little more than corner shops where he would arrive once a month with his nurse and a large pharmacy in the back of his truck. People would line up and wait to be treated. He performed a lot of circumcisions in those years. He would come home once every couple of months for a week. It was a tough life and he finally abandoned the practice after being shot at one too many times in attempted armed robberies.

My father has never been scared to take on a challenge. I vividly remember the time my grandmother decided she wanted a facelift, when we were still living in our small apartment in Poland. Facelifts were not easily accessible under communism, and so my father researched the topic and performed the surgery himself, on our couch. My grandmother was so pleased with the result that, when we came to South Africa, she requested a second one. This time it took place on our dining-room table.

They say that the younger you are, the 'easier' it is to immigrate. When I compare my own experience with that of my younger siblings, I find the opposite to be true. By the time we arrived in South Africa, I had sufficient years of schooling under my belt to slot relatively easily into the unfamiliar education system. This was not the case for my sister and brother, two and five years my junior respectively, whose foundation years had been interrupted by the months we spent in Austria. Yet they adapted. My brother was and still is an extremely social person with the largest group of friends of anyone I know. He forms deep, enduring friendships. It also helped that he was naturally athletic. Skateboarding, hockey and water polo made integration much easier. My sister, the smartest of us all, possesses an uncanny ability to analyse people and situations and find solutions to even the most complex human dynamics. Out of the three of us, she found integration the most challenging. While boys like my brother can fall back on sport, girls often struggle to find commonality beyond a shared history, which leads to tribal behaviour. Neither I nor my sister belonged to a tribe. I was lucky in that I found a group of friends at school that accepted me. My sister only did so at university.

Through it all, however, we had each other. We fought, we made up, we celebrated, we cried. My sister and I shared a room and were both avid readers, which helped with learning English. In my case, my knowledge of English came from reading all the Mills & Boon romance novels I could get my hands on. My sister read more serious novels. Years later, I learnt that my grandmother shared my passion for Mills & Boon romances.

I remember the first time I invited a boy over to the house. My brother and sister positioned themselves outside the window and made monkey noises. That put paid to any further dates at home. Antics aside, theirs are the shoulders I lean on when I'm at my lowest. Both are accomplished. My brother lived in the United Kingdom for a long time, where he was a technical architect for Transport for London and then the technical design authority for the Olympic Games. My sister lived in New York and worked as a film producer and director for Viacom. She filmed promotional videos and interviewed famous people. Both have since joined me at Sygnia, bringing their invaluable skills to the business.

We lost out on a lot of time with our parents during our teenage years and only really reconnected as a family once they retired. Those early years in South Africa were just too turbulent for all of us, particularly my parents, focused as they were on trying to ensure our survival. But we have become a close-knit family since. I feel my mother only really started mothering us when she retired. She took up cooking and always made sure we had something to eat. By that stage, I had given up on the elusive culinary arts, so her home-cooked meals were most welcome. And she was a wonderful babysitter to our children. I would not have had the freedom to pursue my career without her support.

My father used the Covid-19 pandemic to write his memoirs, in Polish, which he self-published as a gift to his children, to document our family history. It was only then that I found out how little he knew about his parents' past and his early childhood.

My parents now live in Cape Town and are ardent followers of Polish politics. They are sanguine about South Africa's political situation and believe they made the right decision to immigrate. If my mother starts to worry, my father tells her to get a glass of wine, sit on the terrace, enjoy the view and not think about it.

When I think about the ebbs and flows of our life together, I realise we all wandered in different directions in those early years, but then drifted back in later years, perhaps making up for the lost time of an interrupted childhood.

It's certainly true that many Polish families who immigrated to South Africa at the same time as us soon returned to Poland. It was just too tough. They missed their country, with all its faults, and they missed the families and friends they had left behind. Language and cultural differences were real obstacles to assimilation. Unlike many, we stuck it out.

On a recent visit to Poland, I saw an incredible one-woman play based on a book by Sabina Baral. In *Zapiski z wygnania* ('Notes from Exile'), Baral recounts her family's emigration from Poland in 1968 due to the ruling communist government's anti-Semitic purge. Her story is my story; our experiences are identical. I have always presented my family's clandestine flight from Poland and subsequent immigration as something interesting that happened in my youth. Baral doesn't. She was traumatised by the events and she says so. She remains traumatised and angry to this day. After seeing the play, I realised that my siblings and I have, over time, romanticised our story. In reality, it was a gruelling and awful time that left deep scars, scars that we hide with humour.

Being twelve and starting school mid-year, in June 1982, meant that I arrived halfway through the last grade of primary school. I was an oddity, but an oddity who excelled in two subjects: mathematics and science. I will be forever grateful to the teacher who took an interest in me and made sure I understood that I had to get into Pretoria High School for Girls (PHSG), the pre-eminent all-girls government high school in Pretoria. Once she explained the zoning issues to me, I managed to persuade my parents to move a few blocks further east in Sunnyside so that my sister and I could qualify for admission.

My years at PHSG were a mixed bag of experiences. As much as it was a government school, it was a school for the privileged. Teenage girls can be a powerful and destructive force of nature, particularly to those who do not fit in. I certainly did not fit in. I had a ragtag group of friends, each of us representing a different nationality. We had fun though, including one infamous trip to Plettenberg Bay, during which a broken-down minivan deep in the Karoo resulted in a kind family taking us in and allowing us to sleep in a room where they stored coffins for future family use. My friends teased me ceaselessly for my 'I never suntan, I never burn' mantra, only to get the worst sunburn of my life.

But I was also subjected to humiliation, as both teachers and girls laughed at me for my foreign accent. A consequence of this was that I learnt to write perfect English, even coming in the top 100 students in the national English Olympiad, but I did not dare speak. But, rest assured, I've made up for it ever since. As my second language, however, the nuances still escape me. I am famous for my malapropisms, or 'magda-propisms' as my colleagues call them, including 'set any lights on fire' instead of 'set the world on fire', 'printing ink by the barrel' instead of 'buying ink by the barrel', and 'long-hanging fruit' instead of 'low-hanging fruit'. To this day I provide my friends and family with plenty of humorous material. Luckily, I've learnt to laugh at myself too.

At PHSG, I also faced denialism for the first time. Some girls made a point of telling me that they believed the Holocaust was a hoax. It was perhaps not surprising, given the censorship of the school syllabus at that time, which omitted the Holocaust and discouraged any references to the existence of the ANC. Sunny South Africa may have replaced gloomy Poland in my life, but corrupt political power was achieved and maintained in the same way. Propaganda was rife. In our matric history exam, the Transvaal Education Department, perhaps aware that their version of history was on its way out, instructed us to answer the questions either as per their approved syllabus or with the correct answers. Marks would be given for both.

I recall that while our history textbook did include references to censored topics such as the history of the ANC, the relevant passages' headings had bracketed warnings making them optional reading if you found the content 'offensive'. The textbook was withdrawn from circulation in 1988, the year after I left school.

In my opinion, good teachers possess unique skills. Teaching should be seen as a calling rather than just a job. The remarkable teachers are those who can inspire and motivate their students. At some stage, I was placed in a history class with a teacher to whom I just could not relate. I truly believed she would destroy my love of history. I made an appointment with the headmistress of the school, a very scary prospect at the time, and in my broken English asked to be moved to another class. To her credit, she complied with my request.

Irrespective of the obstacles I encountered at school, I graduated as the 1987 class valedictorian. But even my valedictory service remains a bittersweet memory. It seemed the headmistress could not accept awarding most of the subject prizes to the Polish refugee. As a result, that year, instead of being awarded to the best student in the subject, certain prizes were awarded to girls who had 'showed the most enthusiasm'.

I recently came across an old school photograph making the rounds on social media. Taken in my matric year, it featured all the girls who bullied me. I toyed with the idea of posting it on Twitter with some scathing comment. But what would be the point? They probably don't even remember me, and they certainly don't realise the impact they had on me all those years ago. I think that's true of all teenage bullies. Everyone has some awful story to tell from their teenage years. Sometimes it is more useful to just forget the past and move forward.

In 2007, I was invited back to PHSG as keynote speaker at the annual graduation ceremony. I prepared a motivational speech for the girls, but

I wrote two openings. The first was the usual, bland 'Thank you to the school for everything I am today', but the second began with 'These were the most miserable years of my life ...' Until I stood on that stage – which I remembered as being giant, but which in fact turned out to be fairly modest in size – I did not know how I would begin. But the truth always wins. I went with the second one. The parents, at least, applauded. When the function was over, shunned by prefects and teachers alike, I was approached by a hoard of girls who were just like I used to be – the ostracised, the marginalised, the misfits – all thanking me for recognising their experiences. That was reward enough. Needless to say, PHSG never invited me to speak there again.

Pretoria in the eighties was a charming and conservative place. Living in the quiet suburbs, surrounded by purple jacaranda trees, there was a perception of safety. I had little understanding of what was going on beneath this facade. Not having grown up in South Africa, the concept of differentiating people by virtue of their skin colour was completely foreign to me. To be honest, I simply did not notice what was happening around us. And a lot was. I remember sitting on the school lawn eating lunch one day when someone came running up, shouting, 'The Mixed Marriages Act has been repealed!' It was 1985, and the Act in question had prohibited interracial marriages and sexual relationships. I stared in confusion as many of the girls jumped for joy. The truth is that our family's exposure to the outside world was fairly limited, with everyone consumed with rebuilding a life, without the luxury of just living one.

Not unusually as children of immigrants, my siblings and I learnt resilience and how to take care of ourselves from a young age. Our parents were just too busy to truly be there for us. And so we became mini adults, making our own decisions about almost everything to do with daily life and learning not to bother our overstressed parents with minor issues.

We only ever received new clothes as birthday and Christmas gifts. Every Saturday morning, we'd go window-shopping in the mall. There were no shopping malls in Poland, so these visits were a real treat and adventure. At fifteen, I was already an aspiring fashionista. As we had no money to indulge my passion, I decided to take matters into my own hands, and got a holiday job at a local supermarket chain. I was placed behind the cold meats and cheese counter, where I quickly learnt to rig the system. Moved by seeing elderly people of limited means come into the store and count out cents to figure out how many slices of ham they could afford to buy, I found a way of always throwing in a few extra slices. No one noticed the 'petty theft'. The money I earned was spent on fashionable outfits. There was the Madonna phase, which involved a lot of pearl necklaces and lace gloves; the *Flashdance* phase of leg warmers with some modern-dance classes thrown in; and the psychedelic phase, when neon yellow was my colour of choice for everything from earrings and necklaces to bracelets and belts. It was the eighties, after all.

Apart from window-shopping, our other frequent entertainment was going to the ice rink in Sunnyside on Saturday afternoons. It's where you went to meet boys. I might have been awkward and provincial, but, coming from Poland, I could ice-skate.

There were two lessons our father taught us through regular repetition. One was that he could give us nothing beyond what he had already given us, namely freedom. We had to use that to make our own way in life. The other, specifically for his daughters, was to never rely on a man and never get into a position where you're 'washing some man's underwear'. Both lessons stuck. While I don't have daughters, my husband and I have passed the first lesson on to our two sons. They must make their own way in life. We have given them a start with an incredible education. Now it is up to them to make the most of it. They have not disappointed us yet.

My parents could not afford to pay for me to go to university. If they had, I probably would have studied medicine. Instead, a friend told me about actuarial science, a complex statistical degree, but one for which life-insurance companies were offering full bursaries to the best students. Without any understanding of either actuarial science or insurance, and without telling my parents, I applied to every life-insurance company I could find for a bursary. I scoured newspaper ads and telephone directories. Eventually, I got an interview with one of South Africa's largest insurance companies, Old Mutual. All credit must go to the first person who took a chance on me, an actuary by the name of Brian Baskir. He interviewed me in Pretoria and clearly saw something beneath the mop of badly cut hair and thick accent. Old Mutual awarded me a bursary to the University of Cape Town (UCT), one of the best academic institutions in South Africa. Fully paid tuition, accommodation, books and even a small living allowance. It was the day that, at the age of eighteen, I became financially independent. I have not taken a cent from anyone since.

5

University

MY HOME LIFE DURING my teenage years was turbulent. Given the multiple stressors and immense pressure they were under, my parents argued a lot. I was looking forward to an escape to Cape Town, but it was not to be. As soon as I announced that I had been accepted to UCT, my father requested a transfer to 2 Military Hospital in Wynberg. And so the family caravan moved down to the Cape and settled in a small house on the wrong side of the tracks in Kenilworth, at the time a suburb on the fringes of acceptability. Fortunately, I had been admitted to one of the best residences at the university, Fuller Hall, so I was at least spared having to live at home as a 'child'. And that is where my life in South Africa truly began. I made friends across the spectrum. I gained the confidence to speak English. And I was finally exposed to the country's politics. It would be untruthful to say that the full horrors were on display. Despite its liberal policies, UCT remained a bubble of mostly white students. Interestingly, however, the bursary schemes run by the insurance companies were quite inclusive. Besides women, they were awarded to students of all races. I thus found myself in the same lecture halls as Thabo Dloti and Sello Moloko, who have since gone on to become two of South Africa's most successful businessmen. It was the start of transformation.

I arrived at UCT in 1988, two years before Nelson Mandela was released from prison. I remember the day of his release – 11 February 1990 – as if it were yesterday. The university was electric. We marched and demanded freedom for all. A referendum on ending apartheid was finally held on 17 March 1992. I still have my original identity document with the stamp of that referendum in it.

As much as UCT gave me a feeling of freedom, arriving at Fuller was a stressful experience. Fortunately, I immediately made friends with a girl who lived across the corridor, and we navigated the complexities of registration together. We are friends to this day. When I reached the front of the queue to register as an actuarial student, Professor Rob Dorrington, famed head of the actuarial science department, took one look at me and asked if there was anything he could do to persuade me to switch to another degree.

Actuarial science was a tough vocation. At our first lecture, Professor Dorrington asked us to look at the person sitting to our right and then our left, and then told us that only one of us would make it through. I was determined to be that one, however difficult actuarial science turned out to be.

To succeed among what was clearly an incredibly intelligent group of people you needed an edge. Mine came about incidentally. My political awakening coincided with my search for my Jewish roots. I made a point of befriending all the Jewish students, who, it transpired, had access to the holy grail: 'the files'. The files contained many years' worth of past actuarial science exam papers and model answers, passed down from generation to generation of students. You had to admire the determination. I was lucky to be fully accepted into the circle of trust. I had a Jewish boyfriend and friends who introduced me to the culture and religion. I learnt to cook kosher food and kept special pans and plates for a particularly observant friend. There was even a stage when I considered full conversion and spoke to a rabbi. The decision came down to having to give up the Christmas tree. That was a step too far.

My years at university were largely spent studying. I did not have anything like the mathematical talent of some of the other actuarial science students. There was no 'working things out from first principles'. You just had to do an example a hundred times until you learnt the formula by heart. It was a humbling experience, but it taught me that no amount of brainpower is a substitute for sheer effort. I wish I had some wild stories to recount, but the truth is that the last time I went to a nightclub was in my orientation week.

Actuarial science attracted some interesting characters. One bright guy figured out how to make a lot of money betting on horses at Kenilworth Racecourse. After upsetting the wrong people, he had to make a run for it, abandoning his bursary. Another one, cracking under the pressure, took up bodybuilding at a time when doctors were experimenting with steroids and using university students as guinea pigs in their medical studies. He transformed from a tall, wiry guy into a hulking great bodybuilder who eventually became one of South Africa's top bodyguards.

My time at university was shaped by three special men who have all contributed to my life in one way or another. There was my boyfriend, who eventually turned his postgraduate thesis into the first socially responsible investment fund in South Africa. A true pioneer in impact investing, he taught me that there is more to life than money through his determination to invest in social good.

Then there was the chess genius, who, struggling to cope with the pressures of being so intelligent, turned to a slightly alternative lifestyle. In third year, we backpacked through Europe together, living in youth hostels and eating one meal a day. It was the first time I had left South Africa since fleeing Poland. I had a budget of thirty US dollars a day and a Eurail Pass that allowed unlimited access to train travel. My friend tried, unsuccessfully, to teach me chess on our train journeys. For me, it was an opportunity to revisit, and appreciate, some of the sights that had passed over my head when my parents took us to Italy. Joined by my boyfriend, we also travelled to Poland, my first visit since we had left in 1981. Since both of them were Jewish, we wanted to go to Auschwitz. Seeing the camp for the first time, buried deep in snow in the middle of winter, was an experience that has remained with me since.

Lastly, there was my closest friend, the sweetest person I have had the privilege to meet and my shoulder to cry on. He was the one I called at two in the morning when I couldn't make my computer work or figure out a project. As a graduation gift, he gave me a Swarovski crystal angel with huge wings and outstretched arms. He told me that one day, when we were both successful, we would each have a glass cabinet full of Swarovski crystals that we'd collected over the years. I now have a large collection in my office, each figure representing a special occasion or celebration. Every day, when I look at it, I think of him.

As I started writing this book, a Polish acquaintance sent me a newspaper article from 1989 that her mother had cut out and kept in a drawer for all these years. Titled 'Polish beauty has plenty of brains', the clipping, aside from recalling an amusing anecdote, provides a snapshot of me as a twenty-year-old. To give some context, for many years Capetonians came together to stage the annual Community Chest Carnival at Maynardville in Wynberg. It was a tremendously popular charity event, featuring funfair rides, family entertainment and food stalls representative of the diverse communities that made up the fabric of the city. One of the items on the programme was the costume competition. The Polish community in Cape Town was tiny and the pool of nominees to represent Poland in the competition even tinier. This particular year, I was somehow persuaded to 'carry the flag'. Dressed in traditional skirts, underskirts, a corset, and more beads than my neck could carry, I was thrust onto the stage. I thanked my lucky stars that the costume, and the flower wreath that came with it, made me unrecognisable.

The competition turned out to be a beauty pageant: Miss International Carnival. I really should have done my research. Astonishingly, I won. I am quoted in the article as saying, 'I don't generally like beauty competitions, all that parading around. This was different, there was a nice spirit, it was for fun, for charity and for something different.' I suspect the reason for my win had less to do with beauty and more to do with the fact that I was the only person who was actually the nationality they purported to represent; all the other contenders were there purely for the pageant and had obviously chosen their 'cultural attire' to gain entry. The competition came with some attractive prizes, including R5 000 – a fortune in those days – and a red beach towel sponsored by Coca-Cola.

The article carries two more notable statements that still ring true for me today. In response to a question about 'boys', I said: 'I tell them that I am studying actuarial science and they are intimidated, they don't want to know me. But if they can't accept me for who I am, forget it.' I still apply this philosophy in the workplace, where I encounter many such men. I refuse to change who I am for a man. Talking about studying, I said: 'You don't have to be incredibly bright to do actuarial science. All it takes is eight to nine hours of work a day, making a lot of sacrifices and giving up the idea of leading a balanced life while you are studying.' This still resonates with me, although I soon learnt that it was not eight to nine hours a day, but more like twelve, as well as weekends and holidays. And it didn't stop when I finished my studies. To be honest, I have never had a holiday. No matter where I go, no matter how exotic, I'm always working. A client who has known me for twenty-five years recently commented that the only thing that changes in my virtual meetings is the background. That basically sums it up.

Winning the contest was not the most humiliating part of the experience, though. The following week, the newspaper printed posters with a photograph of me dressed in Polish national costume, which were attached to every lamppost along the main road running parallel to UCT. I really had to hope that the beads and the flower wreath made me unidentifiable.

In hindsight, undoubtedly the most useful courses I took at university were economics, statistics and accounting. Economics helped me understand world economies and how they work, the role of central banks, and how politics and economics intersect. That knowledge has been extremely valuable in investing, as it assists me in reading the environment and predicting consequences. The reality is that it is the politicians who set economic policies, and politicians have one objective: to get (re)elected. As a result, their decisions are typically short-term in nature.

Statistics taught me how to analyse a wide range of everyday problems. Probability theory has assisted me in a multitude of situations to weigh up the risks and benefits of every decision. It also taught me a more pragmatic approach to life. Some moves are just not worth making.

I did only one semester in accounting, but I wish I had done more. When you run a business, it is essential to understand an income statement and a balance sheet.

It is a great pity that computer science, as taught at university in my day, was too rudimentary to be of any value. Given that we are heading into a future of quantum computing and artificial-intelligence-driven decision-making, research and development, understanding more would have been useful. Instead, I have had to surround myself with people with the relevant know-how. Technological advancements are happening at an astonishing pace.

My one regret is that, being so focused on my studies, I had little time for anything else. I didn't join any clubs or participate in any societies or student forums, apart from being elected as a representative on the Commerce Students' Council (probably because no one else wanted the job). It was a wasted opportunity. University is about so much more than academics. Nevertheless, I had little choice but to study hard. I had a bursary and lived in continual fear that it would be withdrawn if I did not achieve satisfactory marks. I didn't find university easy, but the effort I put in paid off in the long run. I graduated with a business science degree in actuarial science with distinction. I was the fourth person in the history of the department to do so. The first was several years before me, followed by my 'alternative' friend and my then boyfriend. The fifth person to graduate with distinction was a close friend in the year below me. He has since achieved remarkable success on the global stage.

Looking back, I am astounded at how quickly my university years passed. Sadly, I lost touch with most of my university friends, as I did with my friends from high school. Our lives took different paths and I often wonder where they all are. Many left South Africa for 'greener pastures' as part of the first wave of emigration in the mid-1990s. Being an actuary was valuable currency and many only chose the course so that they could find employment overseas. The medical students did likewise. I have touched base with some of them over the years. Very few achieved career success as immigrants, although there are some exceptions. All have one thing to say: 'We did it for our children.' This was the reason my parents used to justify leaving Poland too.

6

Entering the Workplace

A S PART OF MY BURSARY commitment to Old Mutual, I had to work there in the December holidays. This suited me well. I needed the money, as I had no other form of income. (I had already traded my meal vouchers, given to us as part of the bursary, for cash and become an incidental vegetarian, as bread and cheese were cheap.) For the first time in my life, I was exposed to a large corporate culture. Thousands of people working in open-plan offices, row upon row of desks, and status dictated by whether you had one or two visitors' chairs next to your desk, a pot plant and one or two dustbins. I never did figure out the dustbins. There were coffee breaks twice a day in pause areas where everyone complained about the company, their work and their bosses. It was miserable. I had no special skills, so I was relegated to filing. I started to avoid the coffee breaks in favour of playing Tetris on the only colour-screen computer on the floor. At 4 p.m. on the dot, a stampede of people left the building. Anyone trying to get in would have been trampled to death.

It did not take me long to figure out that I did not belong there. I found it depressing that so many people were so unhappy. But I learnt some valuable lessons by listening and observing. I heard stories about what it took to be successful. I noticed that there were no women in senior positions in what was arguably one of the largest employers in South Africa. There was one female actuary, an incredible woman who came to talk to the actuarial students about the work she was doing. She wore lots of jewellery, and I remember deciding there and then that I wanted to be like her. Sadly, she left Old Mutual a few years later having hit one too many glass ceilings.

Perhaps cheekily, but with a nothing-ventured-nothing-gained attitude,

I did some research and discovered that Southern Life, one of the smallest life insurers in the country, had a much more relaxed culture. I phoned their HR department and asked them to take over my Old Mutual bursary, which they did. I was happier there, although small companies also have their failings. They don't always succeed. Southern Life no longer exists, having been bought out by a bigger competitor in 1998.

I graduated from university in 1991. Southern Life then gave me special dispensation to take a year off to self-study full time for the remaining board exams. In those days, actuarial science was made up of two parts: the university degree and board exams set in the UK and known for being particularly tough. I decided to write all three board exams in a single sitting. Unfortunately, I failed one, which meant I would have to spend the following year in purgatory working as an actuarial student as opposed to being employed as a fully fledged actuary. While there were many of us in the same position, I had never failed anything before. My exam setback was a lesson in humility. I learnt that failure is a part of life. You will fail repeatedly. It is not the failure that matters, but rather how you pick yourself up and recover. It took me a couple of months to do so, but, after some tears and a few sleepless nights, I eventually accepted it and just got on with it. When you fail, it is important to surround yourself with like-minded people. I find it helpful to talk through my issues with someone who wants to talk to me about theirs. That way it is not a one-sided conversation. It is a bit of give and take. Everyone has problems; some are bigger than others. It's all relative. Talking to others about what they've experienced or what they're going through can help put things in perspective.

Beginning my working career as an actuarial student rather than a proper actuary was a humbling experience, but one that I value to this day. It meant that I was not elevated to a lofty office and given work I could not handle. Instead, I was thrown into the boiler room and left to learn on my own and by collaborating with others. I can't emphasise enough how important it is to learn the basics of a business. It sets you up for future success. Offices and titles come and go, but skills remain and, ultimately, you are judged based on the skills you have acquired.

In the year that I started working full time at Southern Life, an event happened that threatened to undermine the peace process in South Africa. On 10 April 1993, Easter Saturday, Janusz Waluś, a Polish refugee who had immigrated to South Africa in 1981 (a year before my family), assassinated Chris Hani, the leader of the South African Communist Party. The migrant Polish community was aghast. Waluś was a truck driver and, according to gossip, not very bright. He had somehow become embroiled in far-right politics, aligned with the Conservative Party, which opposed the negotiations to end apartheid. According to the Polish rumour mill, he did not support apartheid per se, but rather feared the communism that had driven his family out of Poland. Whatever his motivation, Waluś was captured and sentenced to death, along with Clive Derby-Lewis, who had instigated the assassination. Both men's sentences were later commuted to life in prison. Derby-Lewis served twenty-two years and died in 2016 while out on medical parole. Waluś remains in prison, the most infamous Pole in South Africa.

It was against this background that I began my first real job, in the 'life product' development department, basically a factory where savings and investment products are invented and manufactured to be sold later to investors. I started with a serious disadvantage. Actuarial science requires detailed knowledge of statistics, mathematics and computer science. With a relatively superficial understanding of statistics and having to ask a colleague how to use spreadsheets, I was not going to set the world on fire.

All actuarial students are automatic members of the Actuarial Society of South Africa, which organised regular conference-style events with different speakers presenting on a variety of topics. Southern Life, apparently still in the dark as to my true mathematical abilities, nominated me to speak about the concept of 'fuzzy logic'. Fuzzy logic is as fuzzy as it sounds. I had no clue what it was and didn't really care to find out. How do you prepare a speech on something you are never realistically going to grasp? As it turned out, this exercise taught me yet another useful skill. I researched the topic and panel beat several academic papers into something that made sense, at least verbally. I then took two days' leave, memorised the speech, stood in front of a long mirror and practised my delivery, over and over again. I rehearsed tone, voice projection and body movement. I learnt a lot in those two days. I am not sure whether my speech taught anyone anything about fuzzy logic, but I conquered my nerves. My advice to any career novice now is to pick a random topic, write a speech, learn it and then practise, practise, practise.

I can't stress enough the importance of learning to speak in public. Growing up in Poland, I participated in regional reading and public-speaking competitions, even winning a couple. This all came to an end when I arrived in South Africa. My thick accent and lack of fluency in English ended any ambitions I might have had to debate in public. I found the orals we had to give at school particularly stressful as I struggled to make myself understood over the sniggering of my classmates. Consequently, the opportunity to present a topic to a large audience so early in my career was invaluable. I have come a long way since the mirror days. Over the course of my career, I averaged over a hundred presentations a year. Today, I never prepare my speeches. I simply ad lib. Whenever I'm asked to give a keynote address that involves giving advice, I raise the topic of giving children the opportunity to learn to debate and present in public as early as possible. Apart from teaching confidence, it is a skill that you will use throughout your life.

My newly acquired skill served me well some time later when I was given the task of doing a roadshow. Southern Life had decided that women deserved their own savings product called Her Own Provider. It was identical to what was offered to men, but the catchy name was meant to attract a brand-new category of savers. The underlying assumption, of course, was that women did not save. As I was the only female actuarial student in the department, I was charged with developing the product and taking it on a roadshow to present to financial advisors. Fortunately, I was able to use the experience and confidence I had gained doing the fuzzy logic presentation to guide me through this. I remember that I bought a white second-hand designer dress for the occasion. I think I spent a month's salary on it. After the first presentation, I went with some colleagues to celebrate at a shawarma restaurant. One of the guys sitting opposite me squeezed his shawarma so hard that he drenched me in thick yellow sauce. He paled when I told him how much my dress had cost. But the story made its way into our collective memory, and to this day it comes up whenever I see one of my former colleagues. Needless to say, I had to throw out the dress.

My first year of formal employment also saw my first activist crusade. I often wonder where the courage – some may say recklessness – came from. Undoubtedly, a big part of it was my background. I grew up in a communist society where everyone was equal. There were few hierarchies. Women were equal to men and were expected to work.

At Southern Life, I had my first encounter with the sexual exploitation of women. It was part of a predatory culture that pervaded the financial services industry in the eighties and nineties. From innuendo to blatant harassment, the full range was on display. My first 'team-building' experience at Southern Life involved the male actuarial students running around undoing the bikini tops of their female colleagues on the beach at a seaside resort. Nude swimming was also encouraged. Later in the day, more 'executives' arrived and, as the alcohol flowed, things got worse. Armed with nothing more than moral indignation, I took the matter to HR. Even in those days my complaint could not be simply dismissed. To be sure, it wasn't taken with a huge degree of seriousness, but I persisted. Our manager, to his credit, held a 'cleansing' workshop, but HR had had enough of me. I was told in no uncertain terms that if I did not stop my campaign, my career would be over before it began.

I backed off, but not because of these threats. Surprisingly (at least to me at the time), I was approached by a delegation of female colleagues who asked me to stop. They told me that they enjoyed dressing up for the men in the office, and if that came with the occasional problematic situation, so be it. There is only one interpretation for this kind of attitude: the women regarded themselves as inferior to men in the workplace. I don't judge the women. I judge the system. In those days, it was really only HR and marketing that were open to ambitious women. A lot has changed since then, and there are many women now trailblazing through the corporate world, but I still encounter brilliant senior women who believe that adopting a flirtatious attitude towards their male counterparts secures them a place at the boardroom table. It does not. If you are doing this to gain recognition and promotion, stop now. Flirting certainly attracts attention, but attention is not the same as being seen as an equal or being taken seriously. Quite the opposite.

Perhaps I could have been more diplomatic in my first battle. What I did was more like picking up a club and bashing people on the head with it, but I do think the situation called for more than mere diplomacy. Despite the outcome, I would not have done anything differently.

On 27 April 1994, in my second year at Southern Life, South Africa held its first democratic election, which resulted in a resounding victory for the ANC. Nelson Mandela became the country's first black president. It was another of those moments one does not easily forget. We all had so much hope for the future. And yet, at Southern Life, transformation was nowhere to be seen, in terms of gender or race. It took a long time for the financial services industry to adjust to the new norm, and even today I think it lags far behind other sectors.

I also went overseas that year. I had a cousin who worked as a stewardess for Luxair, which flew between Johannesburg and Luxembourg once a week. She gave me a free ticket and we flew out to spend a couple of days in Europe together. I will never forget seeing Disneyland Paris for the first time. I was completely overwhelmed by the experience. It was so foreign and yet so magical. On my return, I spent a week describing every attraction to anyone I could corner.

Perhaps unsurprisingly, I did not last long in the actuarial department. Frankly, I found it boring. I have learnt that you need to be passionate about what you do, otherwise your chances of success are slim. Also, your early years should be ones of exploration. I started roaming the corridors of Southern Life looking for opportunities. I spotted one in the investment management division, which was entrusted with making investment decisions on behalf of investors. To be honest, what first caught my attention was the fact that they had the plushest offices. After some persuasion, I was allowed to transfer.

The investment team was composed solely of men who did not really know what to do with me. I was initially allocated to the sales department, but shortly thereafter I was given a new task: developing and managing an index tracking fund. Once again, I was selected based on the amazing mathematical skills everyone assumed I had by virtue of my actuarial qualification. At that time, no one really knew what index tracking was, except that it was a new wave of investing sweeping across the United States. Fortunately, while a complete novice at investing, I was not afraid of a challenge. I hired my first employee, Iain Anderson, who works with me to this day, and together we stumbled and fumbled through the task. At the same time, I got a taste of the male-dominated investment-management scene. It was a lot of tough-looking guys shouting and swearing at one another in the corridors, shifting blame for poor performance, throwing the proverbial knife. There was no concern for the more junior staff or any consideration given to the impact of their behaviour. They did not respect anyone or even care to be respected. It was not an attractive sight. Employees cowered at their desks while these spectacles went on.

This type of behaviour, while inexcusable, could be partially attributed to the enormous amounts of money at stake. Perhaps it is appropriate to pause here and explain investment management in layman's terms. Investment management, at its core, involves investing money by buying and selling shares, bonds or loan notes issued by governments or companies when borrowing money. Most investment managers market themselves as being 'active'. This means that they analyse every company, decide what and when to buy and sell, and thereby grow the money investors have entrusted them to manage. In return, they charge a management fee which is calculated as a percentage of the value of the investments they manage. This can be a very large sum, hence the number of millionaires in the investment management industry and the often overtly aggressive behaviour of those scrabbling to get to the top. I believe that many people in the investment management industry are driven primarily by two emotions: greed and fear. Greed for the monetary rewards associated with being regarded as the best, and fear of losing out or being fired and relegated to the rank of an average person earning an average salary. This does not excuse the behaviour, but it does explain the complex dynamics of the industry.

In 1976, a visionary American investor named John Bogle developed a new, cheaper way of managing money, called index tracking. Two years previously, he had founded what today is one of the largest investment management companies in the world, the Vanguard Group. Bogle's idea was that rather than buying and selling individual companies' shares based on what is at best informed speculation and charging high fees, one could take an index, normally calculated daily by a stock exchange as being representative of the total returns of the stock market on the day, and replicate each and every share in that index in its precise weighting as determined by the stock exchange. The weighting of each company's shares in the index is typically based on the size of the company relative to others. Larger companies therefore have a higher weighting in the index, and thus a greater influence on the performance of the index, than smaller ones.

As an example, if the chosen index is the S&P 500, which represents the performance of the American stock market, you would buy every share in that index and hold it over the long term. Your money will track the performance of the market and you can just forget about it, instead of switching from one investment to another in search of higher returns that never materialise, because decisions are always based on past, not future, performance. Bogle described index tracking funds best when he said, 'The index fund is a practical, cost-effective way to achieve the market's rate of return with little work and price. Individual stocks, market sectors and management selection are all removed from index funds, leaving simply the stock market risk.' He wrote books and articles and gave interviews on the topic. His idea did not make him popular with investment managers, but investors loved it.

I learnt some important lessons reading Bogle's work. First, the average person is best served investing in low-cost funds over the long term. Second, beware of 'star' asset managers and reliance on past performance as an indicator of future success in making investment decisions. Third, do not be impulsive. The latter is essential when markets fall. On seeing negative returns and loss of savings, it is human nature to immediately want to disinvest and put the money in a bank account. This is exactly the wrong decision. Investment markets are cyclical, they rise and fall. Close your eyes through a downturn and ride it out. The market will recover. If you disinvest, you will have zero chance of recovering the lost capital. I wish I had followed my own advice when I invested and promptly disinvested from bitcoin in 2017 after losing a small fortune.

By the 1990s, index tracking was still a novelty, even in the United States. But given that Southern Life's investment management division was failing to deliver good returns and was losing clients by the day, they were ready to try anything. So they sent me on a quest to Los Angeles to learn how to implement it in South Africa. On my return, the first index fund in the country was born, and my love affair with index tracking began, something that has lasted to this day.

At that stage, my work at Southern Life was my sole focus. From a broader perspective, the years under Nelson Mandela seemed stable and inclusive. South Africa hosted and won the 1995 Rugby World Cup. Although not a sports fan, I watched as Mandela, wearing a Springbok rugby jersey, presented the Webb Ellis Cup to South African captain Francois Pienaar in what was widely regarded as a generous gesture of reconciliation and forgiveness. The economy grew after a series of social and economic reforms. By 1996, the country had a new Constitution, vaunted as the most progressive in the world. On the surface, all was well. But I vaguely recall the furore over *Sarafina 2*, when minister of health Nkosazana Dlamini-Zuma authorised her department to award a R14-million contract to Mbongeni Ngema to write a play about AIDS. Despite flaunting tender procedures in what can only be regarded as a giant waste of money, there were no consequences for anyone involved. As the first big corruption scandal to hit the new democratic government, it arguably set the template for what was to follow.

7

Alexander Forbes

Towards the end of 1993, Irene Petrony, widely regarded as the mother hen of all actuarial students in South Africa, set me up on a blind date. Irene worked for Southern Life at the time, and her full-time role was to take care of the actuarial students. She was dedicated to making our lives easier, and after Southern Life ceased to exist she was hired by the Actuarial Society of South Africa to continue her work on its behalf. Every actuary in the country knows Irene, and she, in turn, knows every actuary. Simon Peile was also an actuary, and already a senior executive at Alexander Forbes. To say we did not hit it off is putting it mildly. He thought I was arrogant and I thought he couldn't stop bragging about himself. But Irene firmly believed we belonged together. A few months later, knowing that I was looking for an apartment, she organised a viewing for me. I was met at the door by the owner – to my surprise, it was Simon. Let's just say, I never left, but I did change his navy and maroon colour scheme.

The fact that we are both actuaries could have made for a very boring relationship. Fortunately, neither of us is a conventional actuary. Simon is a bit of an adventurer. Early on in his actuarial career, he took a seven-year sabbatical to travel the world and lead overland expeditions through Africa and South America. This meant he had an arsenal of interesting stories to tell that had little to do with mathematics and statistics. He had also worked in the United Kingdom and Australia before deciding to return to Cape Town to settle down. When I met him, he was a keen kayaker who had kayaked the Grand Canyon in the United States. In the early days, to impress him, I bought all the gear and pretended that I wanted to take up kayaking. The pretence lasted for exactly one trip down the freezing Breede River. I also took up golf. With my shiny new gear, I was the envy of every golfer sitting and drinking on the terrace of the clubhouse. That is, until I dug up the tee like a mole and retreated in shame, never to pick up a golf club again.

The only sport-based activity that we both enjoyed was cycling. But even that did not come without some turbulence. On one of our first dates, Simon invited me for a cycle ride from Camps Bay, along the ocean, all the way to the top of Chapman's Peak with its sweeping views of Hout Bay. It was late afternoon and I was a bit of a novice on a racing bike. When we turned around, Simon cycled well ahead, leaving me to make my way back to Camps Bay alone as the sun set and night fell. He did come back to look for me in his car, but it took a while before I accepted another date.

Unsurprisingly, being an adventurer, Simon is not a lover of urban living. On our first anniversary as a couple, I organised a romantic trip through the capitals of Europe. The first stop was Paris. Instead of showing his appreciation, Simon walked into the first supermarket he saw, bought wine, cheese and baguettes, sat down in the shade of the trees alongside the Champs-Élysées and made it clear that he was not moving. I didn't speak to him for a day, but I also learnt not to force him to be someone he wasn't.

After a year and a half of dating, in July 1996, Simon proposed on the shores of Mumbo Island in the middle of Lake Malawi. Predictably, I first had to kayak there through fairly choppy waters. We have since seen the island ranked repeatedly as one of the most romantic places in the world.

Our engagement was a bit of a cultural eye-opener for me. Simon's parents organised an engagement party in England to coincide with the family's annual pheasant-shooting weekend. Simon has a large family in the UK, and over the years the annual pheasant shoot became a way of bringing everyone together. With the shoot taking place in the morning, the engagement party was scheduled for lunchtime. As we waited for everyone to arrive, we received the awful news that one of Simon's uncles had passed away of a heart attack. In Polish culture, this would have meant a lot of wailing and tears. But in British culture, it meant that his wife and daughters arrived at the engagement party as if nothing had happened. Astounded, I was told that it would have been extremely bad manners to ruin our event and that the time for grief would come later.

Towards the end of 1995, I was feeling the tension at Southern Life. Despite enjoying the work, I decided to seek greener pastures. Around this time, Simon and I were invited to a dinner with Leon Lewis, one of Alexander Forbes's larger-than-life joint chief executive officers. At the time, every actuary wanted to work for Alexander Forbes. Its prestige was largely thanks to Leon and his co-CEO, Graeme Kerrigan. They had taken a small business and built it into an impressive independent consulting firm, advising South Africa's largest retirement funds on how to design retirement benefit strategies for their employees. I had never met Leon, but as a senior executive in the Cape Town office, Simon had told me that he prided himself on intimidating others in the boardroom by playing with his giant gold Rolex watch.

As we sat at the table, I strategically positioned myself next to Leon. I had a plan. One of the skills I have perfected over the years is getting what I want while making the other person think it was all their idea. It is a fine art and has as much to do with the way you present an idea as with your tonality and mimicry. Never ask directly for something that seems unachievable. Rather guide the person's thinking towards what you ultimately want. I started with industry small talk, to show I knew my stuff, then subtly shifted the conversation to highlight my skills and finally to praise the achievements of Alexander Forbes. By the time I was finished, Leon had no doubt that Alexander Forbes and I were a perfect fit. I walked away with a job offer.

And that's how, in January 1996, I started working at Alexander Forbes. I was tasked with starting an investment consulting division to advise retirement funds on how best to invest their money for the long term. I worked with another actuary based in Johannesburg. Between us, we came up with the framework, the service offerings and the marketing strategy. Within a year we had formed the division and acquired some large appointments. This was my first taste of starting a business. To this day I cannot believe that the chief financial officers of companies such as Shell and BP took advice from a twenty-six-year-old telling them how to invest their billions. I attribute this to the fact that I was one of the first female actuaries in South Africa. My qualifications gave me a huge amount of credibility. People saw beyond my age and took me seriously. I often do presentations to actuarial students and they always ask the same question: Is the hard work worth it? My answer is always a resounding yes. While I never enjoyed the actual work of an actuary very much and got out as soon as I could, having a credible degree behind me was the tailwind to my success. You do not need to be a practising actuary to be successful, but earning that degree can be the key that opens doors in the future.

At Alexander Forbes, I honed my marketing and sales skills. As an investment consultant I was always the observer in the room, guiding decision-making on which investment managers the retirement funds should appoint, but never being part of the actual decision. After I left Southern Life, there were no index tracking managers left, so all anyone had to go on were the outward skills of active managers. I soon observed that, despite my guidance, two investment management companies kept winning all the new business tenders. One was a life insurance company with a small investment management division, which no longer exists. Their marketing team brought the first Proxima video projector to South Africa as a marketing tool. Until then, everyone had only ever used overhead projectors, antiquated machines that involved manually placing pre-printed 'transparencies' onto a glass surface with a light source below it. The Proxima was such a hit that this company became regarded as the most tech-savvy in the country and the money followed. The other company had a shrewd CEO who sent two extremely good-looking men in to pitch. Wearing designer suits, double-cuffed shirts and silk ties, a first in the financial services industry, they stood out from the crowd of largely grey-suited salesmen in brown shoes. Irrespective of their investment performance, these two companies got the bulk of new business appointments. Appearances and innovation matter. It may seem superficial, but sometimes, to a layperson faced with a complex industry filled with jargon and an intangible product, optics are all they have to go on.

One other thing that stood out was that there were no women representing investment managers. The industry has changed a bit since those days, but not enough.

Simon and I got married a few months into my stint at Alexander Forbes. As neither of us had any money, the wedding was done on a budget. We tied the knot on 16 March 1997 in a picturesque stone church opposite the world-famous Kirstenbosch National Botanical Garden. We had a small reception with family, friends and my favourite flower, Gerbera daisies.

Our first house was a glass box on the slopes of Lion's Head. We had a spectacular view of Table Mountain and a large mortgage bond to pay off. Simon's aunt, an incredible woman who made a lot of money on the stock markets while working as a nursing assistant, gave us the money for the deposit. We loved the house. It was the perfect setting for entertaining, but it would become a hugely impractical extravagance when we had our first child.

By mid-1997, it had become clear to me that all the real power at Alexander Forbes resided in Johannesburg, the business centre of South Africa, and that the Cape Town office was a poor satellite. Once again, I began to cast about for opportunities. This time, the opportunities found me. Three different investment management companies approached me with job offers at the same time. The smallest of these – Coronation Fund Managers – was barely four years old, having been launched by a bunch of investment managers who left a larger company. I'd had a bit of a run-in with them previously. I found their presentations to my clients so amateurish that I'd called their senior fund manager and told him that Alexander Forbes would no longer support them as their fumbling was an embarrassment. That same fund manager called me out of the blue one day and asked me to lunch. After an hour-long marketing monologue in which he talked about Coronation's move to new offices, I decided to take matters into my own hands.

'Are you offering me a job or are you asking for my interior design advice?' I asked with the confidence of youth.

It turned out it was the former. I was intrigued, even though I would have to take a third of my former salary with the promise of a 'bonus'. At that stage, the risk was magnified because I carried financial responsibility for my parents and my extended family in Poland. I agreed to an interview, which was conducted by a panel of executives, led mostly by the head of investments.

'Why should we hire you?' was the first question they fired at me.

'Wrong question,' I replied. 'Why should *I* join *you*?'

8

The Coronation Years

I BEGAN WORKING AT CORONATION on 1 September 1997. I was the fourteenth employee in what was essentially a start-up.

Founded in 1993, Coronation was a small boutique investment fund manager with not a lot going for it. They focused on managing the assets of retirement funds. To be fair, they had managed to attract a few clients based on their reputation and performance, successes largely ascribed to their very charismatic CEO. But on the day I joined, Coronation let go of him without explanation. In a twist of fate, the fund manager who I had lambasted when I was at Alexander Forbes and who had offered me the job at Coronation was made the new CEO. Although he bore the official title, it soon became clear that the person running the show was the head of investments.

My decision to join Coronation was made easier by the fact that the other two job offers came from companies that I instinctively knew wouldn't be a good fit for me. The first was from a large insurer similar to Southern Life. The second was from an aggressively male-dominated investment bank where I just knew that, as a woman, I would get nowhere. While the Coronation team's early wild years were behind them by the time I joined, it was still a mostly white male environment. There were nude posters and cheeky screensavers scattered around the office. In my first three months, I decided one weekend to clean up the smut. Armed with a collection of Anne Geddes pictures, I replaced every nude poster and screensaver in sight with sweet baby faces framed by flower petals. (Those were the days before password protection.) On Monday, no one said a word. But both the Anne Geddes babies and the naked ladies had disappeared, or at least gone underground.

My job description was vague. I was basically charged with taking care of everything related to the retirement fund clients. Coronation's attitude amounted to 'we don't really understand retirement funds, you handle it'. I managed everything, from product design, marketing and business development, to the legal side of things, quantitative analysis, client servicing and administration. It is not difficult to become a jack of all trades in a small shop, particularly if you are willing to do the things that no one else wants to do. I was that person. The weekends and holidays disappeared as I focused on building the company and gathering assets. I travelled across South Africa in rented cars with a map on my lap. I visited the most obscure locations, from industrial factory settings to semi-rural villages, anywhere where there was a company with a retirement fund willing to invest money. I was young and driven – I didn't give any thought to the obvious safety concerns for a woman traversing the country alone. Those initial years at Coronation were exhilarating. My first bonus was bigger than a year's salary at Alexander Forbes. I bought a new electric-blue Toyota Rav4, my first real car, and thought I had made it.

Simon and I had planned on starting a family, but I didn't know that I was already pregnant when I joined Coronation. As soon as I found out, I had to let them know. 'Yet another typical woman,' I overheard one shareholder, a man with little compassion or passion for anything but money, say to the head of investments – presumably meaning he thought I would disappoint in terms of how much energy I would put into my work. Well, I was going to prove them wrong. I didn't let the pregnancy stop me. To limit weight gain, I went to spinning classes in oversized T-shirts to hide my bump and travelled on aeroplanes up to the eighth month. No one questioned that.

Simon and I went to prenatal classes to prepare. We inadvertently chose a course that advocated natural childbirth at home with a midwife. At our last class, the instructor took a roll call. How many couples were going with natural childbirth? Everyone except us put up their hands. She looked at us disapprovingly. A month later, we had a class reunion. The instructor did another roll call. How many women had had natural childbirth with no anaesthetic? I was the only one to put up my hand.

Our son Alex was born on 5 May 1998. By the time he arrived, I had a lot on my plate at Coronation. I was unprepared for the challenges of juggling a new baby and a new job. After a week of the CEO calling me multiple times a day with questions, I gave up on maternity leave, packed Alex into a bassinet and took him to work with me. The ladies at Coronation took care of him while I attended meetings. For the rest of the time, he sat on my desk, quite content, as I worked away. I eventually found a nanny, and Alex resumed life as a homebound infant. This is one of the things I regret. I wish I had spent more time with my children when they were young. I made up for it subsequently, but you can never get those years back. I also regret not having more children than I did, a whole bunch to fill the house with laughter. At the time, I didn't feel I had a choice. I was either going to be one of the men or a 'typical woman', easily dismissed.

I guess I proved myself to be atypical, as I was soon asked to join Coronation's board of directors. Once again, I was the only woman in the room. I was twenty-seven years old.

Coronation as a company really began to take off. In 1998, we opened offices in Dublin, and in 1999 in London. As business picked up, so did the volume of work on my desk. My first hire, a quantitative genius named Willem van der Merwe, and my personal assistant, Ronel Bantjes, became an indispensable support team. They would move with me over the years, from company to company, and stayed on well after I started my last venture.

As the work intensified, I never said no. I never complained. I think this is one of the primary differences between men and women. Men demand recognition, and they do so verbally. Women expect recognition to come to them. We firmly believe that others will notice our efforts and reward us. We suffer in silence. Unfortunately, most companies do not care unless you demand that they do so. They are happy to pile on the work. I wish I had spoken up more, been more assertive about the volume of work given to me, hired more people, delegated more. Instead, I sacrificed weekends, evenings, holidays. Few men would do that. And yet they thrive. Some of what I did was a function of being a woman, some was born out of a belief that I needed to work hard to succeed, and some was due to the pressure of having people who depended on me financially. Whatever my reasons, it was a tough education. While my friends were out partying and enjoying being young, I was carrying the weight of the world on my shoulders. And it really wasn't necessary.

Coronation's culture shifted over time, as tends to happen with any rapidly growing business. What started as an entrepreneurial enterprise became a money-printing machine. We were constantly told that we were the 'owners' of the business and had to behave as such. We believed the marketing shtick. I have since learnt that unless you own physical shares in a business, you are not an owner. You remain an employee at someone else's mercy. It does not matter how attractive the salary, the bonus or the share option pool; you are an employee.

The investment team filled out with more young people. There was one female fund manager, but she was never treated as a senior. Then the infighting began. Part of it had to do with how remuneration was heavily tilted towards biannual bonuses. We were paid very low basic salaries, even by today's standards, but the bonuses made up for it, as well as being a reward for good performance. The bonus pool was limited, however, and you had to fight for your share. That was the men's world. In my experience, women shy away from confrontation about money. It did not help matters that the CEO and the head of investments used what I perceived to be a 'divide and rule' strategy, to ensure that the rest of the company never united against them and the fact that they received the lion's share of the pool. Infighting was encouraged, subtly at first via friendly gossip about other team members, but more aggressively as the bonus pool got larger.

While running a business based on low salaries and high bonuses might seem appealing to any entrepreneur, there are risks involved for the staff. An incident at Coronation taught me the value of having appropriate risk and disability insurance in place in case something happens to prevent you from earning a living. Usually, the premiums you pay and the potential benefits you receive are linked to your salary. At Coronation, with our low salaries, those benefits were negligible. No one paid attention until one senior staff member lost his leg in a fight with his girlfriend. Supposedly by accident, she reversed her car instead of going forwards and squashed his leg between two bumpers. We all realised that should he not be able to return to work, he would have little to rely on.

My experience at Coronation changed as the bonus pool grew. I was one of the four most senior executive members of the team, and the only woman. Being so hands-on, I understood the business inside out. I did not realise just how threatened the CEO felt by that. Whatever feelings I brought up in him, I have over the years brought up in other men. Not many, to be fair, but definitely some. It is a visceral hatred of what women can achieve. There is no logic behind it. There is no fairness to it. It is just there and has to be expressed. And here is where women are at a huge disadvantage to men. In my experience, women are not naturally aggressive. For the most part, we are emotional, passionate and collaborative. We seek consensus, stability and happiness. This means that an environment which is none of these things immediately destabilises our psyche. I think this is what lies at the core of why there are so few senior women in the financial services industry. We don't have the requisite skills to fight like men do. I certainly did not fight. I worked.

Having said that, what happened to me as Coronation grew went beyond what anyone should have to experience in a workplace.

As part of the bonus allocation, we were called in by either the CEO or the head of investments for a biannual performance evaluation. Mine was always with the CEO. As I recall it, he would open each discussion by saying that we were not there to discuss my performance, as my performance was excellent. We were there, he said, to discuss why everyone at Coronation hated me and how hard he had to defend me every time. For a man, being told what others think of him is a non-starter. Performance is the only thing that matters. He would not be distracted by emotion-tugging nonsense when negotiating for money. Women, however, are different. For us, it matters what others think. Particularly if you believe you've given it your best. What followed this opening salvo can only be described as abuse.

The CEO would list my failings as a human being until he broke me. If it took half an hour, he would dedicate half an hour to the task. If it took longer, so be it. The process would last until I was in tears and barely coherent. This, of course, meant that I was in no position to negotiate my bonus. I took what I got with gratitude. A senior fund manager who still works at Coronation witnessed one of these sessions. He came out of that meeting pale, but he did not defend me or stand up for me.

For years I told myself that this was merely a negotiating ploy used by men to pay women less. And there is some truth to that, but it goes deeper. Some men truly believe that no woman can be seen to be better, stronger or wiser than a man, and that men must dominate. Any threat to their control is met with rage. And I was the target of the Coronation CEO's rage.

It usually took me three or four days to recover from one of these sessions and then I just got on with it. I would work harder; I would prove him wrong. Little did I know or realise that what was happening had nothing to do with me and everything to do with him and how I made him feel.

In telling this story, I am not looking for sympathy. I am often asked why I stayed, given my experiences. The answer is complicated, ranging from my emotional entanglement in building Coronation and having a family to support financially, to a sort of Stockholm syndrome. I resigned twice, and was convinced to come back both times.

In hindsight, I should have walked out and never looked back. But life is never that simple. As I've said before, you make some good and some bad choices. The choice to stay was mine and mine alone, and I must take responsibility for my part in enabling that behaviour. The choice to stay was a bad one. Over time it took its toll on my confidence and my health. I developed chronic insomnia, I started to suffer from panic attacks and anxiety. I developed rheumatoid arthritis, which is mostly ascribed to stress. I overcompensated by dissociating from my physical environment and over-exercising. None of that should be a function of the workplace. But I don't blame the CEO or Coronation for my health problems; I blame myself for not breaking the cycle sooner.

That CEO went on to have three daughters and no sons. A few years ago, at a charity function in Stellenbosch, I was accosted by a woman who looked vaguely familiar. She dragged me to her table as she wanted to show me something. I finally recognised her as my former CEO's wife. She picked up her phone and proudly showed me photographs of her three daughters, all beautiful, all accomplished. If I remember correctly, one was a chartered accountant, one a lawyer and the other a medical doctor. As she scrolled through the photographs, she told me that I was a hero in their home, that to her daughters I represented everything a woman could accomplish. I looked down at the bent head of my ex-boss, sitting at the table, listening as his wife extolled the virtues of the woman he had detested. I'm a great believer in karma.

Compared to the biannual bonus negotiations, the team-building strategy sessions were relatively mild affairs, with one exception. One of the first I attended required everyone to have a psychological profile done ahead of time. These profiles were then plotted on a four-quadrant grid. Everyone wanted to be in the same quadrant as the CEO, who, unsurprisingly, had achieved a clear alpha-male placement. Fights broke out as people jostled for positions and argued about the accuracy of the testing.

The years went by in a whirl. My second son, Nicholas, was born on 2 June 2000. This time I did not even bother mentioning maternity leave. I scheduled an induction for Thursday evening and went back to work on Monday morning. No one blinked. Such was the life of a woman trying to succeed in a man's world.

It was around this time that both the CEO and CFO turned forty. The CEO's personal assistant collected money from all the staff for a gift. None of us knew what it would be, but something nagged at me, so I asked her. She looked slightly sheepish when she told me that she had hired a stripper to come to the office during the executive management meeting. I was horrified and told her to cancel and get a refund. Of course, the stripper refused to refund the money. We needed a plan B. The stripper described herself as a Sharon Stone lookalike, so I suggested that she turn the event into a kissogram. She was to come in, kiss both men on the cheek and hand them some 'Happy Birthday' balloons. It sounded like a reasonable compromise.

I placed a female scout team in reception to screen her when she arrived, as I couldn't miss the management meeting. At midday, the boardroom door swung open and a fifty-something woman in black leather gear marched in holding a boombox and a giant balloon. So much for Sharon Stone. When the CEO saw her, he literally bolted for the door. I have never been so embarrassed in my life.

All of this happened while a scandal was brewing in South African politics. In the late 1990s, rumours started circulating about the costly armaments deal that the government was negotiating. It had been sold to the public as a necessary modernisation of the country's defence force. In 1999, R30 billion was spent on defence equipment, including submarines, fighter aircraft and helicopters. The procurement was soon followed by news of corruption and bribery that incriminated senior government figures, including then deputy president Jacob Zuma. Independent investigations by the United Kingdom and the United States resulted in a number of multinational companies being fined, while a sham commission of inquiry back home exonerated Zuma and his cronies. The companies that benefited at the expense of the poor in South Africa included DaimlerChrysler Aerospace, BAE Systems, Saab and Thomson-CSF, now known as Thales.

That same year, 1999, Thabo Mbeki succeeded Nelson Mandela as president of the country. Mbeki will be remembered for his HIV/AIDS denialism, which contributed to the unnecessary deaths of over 300 000 South Africans. Mbeki never apologised for his views and their consequences. It was only when Kgalema Motlanthe succeeded him as president in 2008 that government's approach to treating HIV was reversed from promoting garlic, beetroot and lemon juice to rolling out antiretroviral drugs. Despite these basic human rights abuses, it was business as usual in South Africa. Many of us remained optimistic about the future. Those who did not, emigrated.

———

My stint at Coronation ended abruptly and unexpectedly. From the time we opened the overseas offices, Coronation's shareholders had little appetite for putting real capital behind any new venture. Consequently, the offshore operation hobbled along, as it does to this day. You can't build a business without making some financial sacrifices.

In late 2002, it was suggested that I move to London to run Coronation's struggling business. I accepted the challenge and signed the new contract of employment with excitement. My husband resigned from his job at Alexander Forbes with three months' notice and was put on a year's 'gardening leave', which meant he could not work in South Africa. We started making plans for our relocation, looking at schools for the children, and so on. At this time, the head of investments came to me and said that despite relocating to London, I would still need to retain all my responsibilities for the institutional business in South Africa as it could not function without me.

Then, in early 2003, Coronation Fund Managers was unbundled from its owner, Coronation Holdings, and the shareholders decided to list the 'new' company separately on the Johannesburg Stock Exchange (JSE). This came as a surprise to us all. The listing had to happen quickly for a number of reasons, and rumours soon began to spread that both the CEO and the head of investments had agreed with the main shareholder that they would receive shares in the newly listed Coronation Fund Managers, leaving out everyone else. I was probably the only person who did not believe the rumours. I asked the two executives several times whether they had done such a deal and whether we could organise something for all the staff. Each time they denied that they had been allocated any shares. They even told me they had tried to do something for everyone, but that the shareholders had been unwilling.

Around this time, the CEO invited me to breakfast one morning. I went with no expectations. He seemed agitated and told me that there could be only one CEO of Coronation and that, after discussing it with the shareholders, they had agreed that it would be him. I didn't understand why he was telling me this. It only became clear a few years later when I was told that there had been some discussion about who would run the newly listed Coronation, him or me. I am not sure if that was true or not, but the breakfast certainly made no sense at the time.

A consequence of the listing was that my move to London was put on hold. As I was involved in drafting the listing documentation, emails were constantly circulating between me, the majority shareholder, the CFO and the CEO. One such email came with a trail. I noticed that some of the emails in the chain were unfamiliar, so I scrolled to the bottom where I found an email written by the majority shareholder to the CEO. In summary, it set out that the shareholder had made four per cent of Coronation's shares available to staff, and it was up to the CEO to decide who the key staff at Coronation were. The CEO's reply, as I recall it, was that there were only two key people at Coronation, himself and the head of investments, and that he would make sure that everyone else toed the line.

I was astounded. The betrayal I felt was enormous. With hindsight and the benefit of years of experience, I probably should not have been that surprised. Greed clouds people's judgement. I printed out the email and left it on my desk for a few days as I absorbed the contents. Finally, I could put it off no longer. I called the CEO and the head of investments into a meeting to ask them one last time whether they had struck a separate deal for themselves and whether the majority shareholder and thereby the owner of Coronation had refused to do anything for the staff. Once again they denied it. Slightly theatrically, I pulled out the email and asked them to explain it. Their faces turned to stone and the head of investments told me to forget what I had seen. The two of them had been there at the beginning, he said, and none of the rest of us had – we were all employees, and that is all we would ever be. Well-paid employees, but just employees. It was a harsh lesson in the difference between being an owner and an employee. Ultimately, it does not matter who does the heavy lifting. It only matters who owns the shares.

I left the meeting shell-shocked. The news of their shareholding would be made public in the pre-listing statement to potential shareholders. It was only a matter of time before everyone knew the truth. The next morning, I walked into the CEO's office and told him I wanted to resign. He asked me to put it in writing. I pulled a tissue from a box on my PA's desk, wrote 'I resign' on it, and walked out with my personal laptop and a box of possessions. The adrenaline rush lasted for about twenty minutes, and then the panic set in. I remember driving away thinking, *What have I done?* Simon was on gardening leave. We had financial obligations. And now I was thirty-one and unemployed. I didn't sleep that night. The CEO had asked me to return the next morning to fill out the official paperwork.

The following day, ignorant of labour law and my rights, I drove back to Coronation for a final meeting with the CEO. For the last time, he unleashed a tirade on me. I remember being told that everyone was celebrating that I was leaving, that no one would miss me, that I was utterly replaceable and had in fact already been replaced, and not to expect a farewell function. He carried on until I was broken and in tears. In that state, I signed what turned out to be a mutual termination of employment agreement, which I now know meant that I would have no legal claim against Coronation for anything. I drove away in tears.

When I was calmer, I read the agreement. In addition to having ceded all my rights, I saw that the agreement also included a six-month restraint-of-trade clause, which meant I could not work for six months in the financial services industry. Unemployment loomed. I phoned him for an explanation, as well as to ask how he would like me to handle the hand-over. Before I could get to that part, he told me to read what I signed in future, and hung up. Wise counsel. As he clearly was not interested in an orderly handover, I deleted all the work I had ever done for Coronation from my laptop. Interestingly, no one ever asked me for any of that information, or any explanation. Just as easily as I deleted the data, so I was deleted from the annals of Coronation. Perhaps the best explanation is that 'read what you sign' applies both ways. As much as I had no claim on Coronation, they knew they had no claim on me.

This was the end of my chapter at Coronation, but the beginning of an incredible journey of discovery, learning, independence and success. I took numerous lessons from the Coronation years, many of which have shaped everything I've done since. The clearest one was that women have to work harder than men to succeed. I struggled to compete with male aggression in the workplace and to voice my opinions. I almost always came off worse in a verbal fight, and I know many women have had the same experience. I don't know if there's a solution, but there are tools and coping mechanisms that women can use and develop. One of the most important skills I learnt was to speak clearly and confidently, to use the power of my voice. One of my coping mechanisms, which I'm sure psychologists would criticise, was a type of dissociation. When discussions got heated I learnt to picture myself in a Perspex box. Nothing said in the meeting could upset me – the words would simply bounce off the walls of my personal space. Over the years, this helped me to remain calm and collected in meetings, and ensured I never lost focus. Another skill I picked up was to always make sure I knew more about a subject than anyone else. I would use every awkward pause in a conversation to throw in extra information with confidence. I also learnt not to take anything personally. If someone gets personal with you, it's usually a reflection on them and not you. As women, we need to develop the scales of a pangolin.

Looking back on those years, there are things I should have done differently. I did not have to work as hard as I did. Given my senior position, I could have asked for more resources and delegated more. Delegation and management are two skills that are essential to success and better learnt early on. Delegation does not mean outsourcing your own work to others just to take credit for it later. Instead, it means using your skills to guide others to achieve the outcome you want. The responsibility for that outcome remains with you. Better delegation in the Coronation years would have allowed me to balance my work and family life. I could have spent more time with my children and husband. I could have been less stressed. It is fine to make mistakes. No one is perfect. The importance of mistakes is to learn from them and not repeat them.

I could have placed fewer expectations on my shoulders. Yes, I wanted to achieve. But I did not have to do so by competing with others. It should also not have come at the expense of my health. I should have had more confidence in the quality of the work I delivered. Confidence, particularly at a young age, is often difficult to come by. I certainly could have negotiated harder for my bonuses. I knew that my male colleagues earned more than me, and yet I never brought that up in any of my bonus discussions.

Finally, I could have – *should have* – walked away earlier from what was obviously a toxic situation. Walked away and never looked back. Based on my experiences, I firmly believe that walking away and looking for greener pastures is not failure. In fact it is a sign of personal strength.

9

Motherhood and Family

I ACHIEVED A LOT IN my time at Coronation, but it came at a cost to not only me, but also my family. Both my boys were born while I was working there and I missed out on so much during their early years. I'm often asked by other women: Can I have it all as a woman and achieve balance, and can I lead a fulfilling life? The answer to the first is a resounding no, but an emphatic yes to the second. A man's life, for the most part, is simple and linear. Traditionally, a man gets up in the morning expecting his breakfast to be made and shirts to be ironed. He goes to work where he can focus without interruption: he doesn't have to worry about phone calls from school, unexpected medical appointments or organising a plumber to fix the tap. He comes home to a warm meal and to relax in front of the TV with a glass of wine or a beer. A woman, however, is a juggler. She is expected to shop, maintain a clean home, organise repairs, supervise the children and their homework, attend school meetings, drive the children to parties and after-school activities, make time for exercise, look good, iron those shirts, cook those meals, and then possibly still have a career. Just writing this makes me feel exhausted.

So, no, as a woman you cannot have it all and achieve balance. What you can do is choose your priorities. What is important to you? Is it having a career or being a mother? There are no wrong answers. Each option comes with its rewards and sacrifices. Once you have chosen – if you have a choice, of course – give up or outsource the activities that make you unhappy or take up too much time. If you're lucky enough to be married to someone willing to lean in, so much the better. I outsourced driving the kids to school to Simon and cooking to a housekeeper, and I did not attend school functions unless my children were performing. Do I have regrets? Of course, plenty of them. I wish I had spent more time with my children when they were little. I wish I had learnt to be a better cook. I wish I had not been welcomed as a 'new' mother at the handful of school functions I did attend – it got boring after eighteen years. But those were the consequences of the choices I made.

When Alex started primary school, he was exposed to the concept of the stay-at-home mother and all the warmth and benefits that brought. He came to me as a seven-year-old and announced, very seriously, that when he gets married one day, his wife is not going to have to work. Instead of letting it be a dagger in my heart, I sat my sons down and said, 'Guys, I will never be the mother who attends parent–teacher meetings, bakes cookies and takes you to parties in the middle of the afternoon. But one day, when you are older and need advice, I want to be the first person you turn to for that advice, as I would have lived through what you are facing and can offer words of wisdom.' They accepted this and dealt with it. Today they say they never noticed my absence, but I am sure at the time it was less than ideal. Simon and I once overheard a discussion between the boys in which Nicholas asked Alex who was the 'boss' in mum and dad's relationship. Alex's answer was simple: 'Mum is the boss at work and Dad is the boss at home.'

One of my great advantages was my husband, Simon. When I'm asked the secret of a woman's career success, I always answer: Marry the right man. To succeed, you need support. You need someone who will be there for you, someone to listen when you need to offload, someone to share the housework without complaint, someone who will not feel threatened by your success. It takes a very strong man to marry a strong woman. I have been lucky.

To his credit, Simon has never complained about my life choices. He eventually joined me on my journey when we started a series of companies together, including Sygnia. We did have some ground rules, though. All successful marriages are based on compromise and having time to oneself. This is difficult in a normal marriage, and doubly so when you work together. One of the tools we employ is giving each other the time and space to do the things we enjoy as individuals. Simon loves bird-watching in foreign destinations, the more exotic and unspoiled the better. He lives for his 'life list', which is birder-speak for the list of unique birds he has seen in his lifetime. His is currently 4500 species long, placing him approximately 250th out of the 500000 birders on the global birders' record-keeping service. He makes an average of three trips a year to places most of us would never think of visiting. He comes home covered in insect bites and sporting marks left by leeches on his shins. His most unpleasant encounter was with chiggers deep in the forests of Mexico. They are worth googling.

I have never begrudged him his hobby. I think that for a marriage to succeed, you have to differentiate between the things you can change about each other and those you can't, and accept it. When we were younger, and before online shopping was invented, I would travel to London to shop, arriving with three empty suitcases and leaving with excess baggage. Early on in our marriage, Simon made it abundantly clear that he does not 'do shopping' and never will. So that became my downtime. Of course, you also need to do enjoyable things together. We travel. It's as simple as that. We can make a spur-of-the-moment decision and be in another country within two days. All that we need is a packed suitcase and a good travel agent. As marriages go, and with twenty-five years of togetherness behind us, we lead a very happy life.

I often wonder what brought us together and keeps us together. Undoubtedly, one of the factors is that we are so different, we complement each other. I joke that he brought the adventure, whereas I brought the drama. I have always been able to rely on Simon's calm approach to problem-solving. We never want for conversation and often wonder about those couples who sit in restaurants not speaking to each other. Everyone is different, but my best ideas come to me when I am talking, rather than thinking. Having someone who listens to me, and who understands my world, has made all the difference.

As far as parenting is concerned, we made sure we spent quality time with our children, in spite of our demanding workloads. We were fortunate to have the means to build a holiday house in a coastal town about an hour's drive from Cape Town, and we spent some magical holidays there, particularly at Christmas and Easter when the whole family gathered to celebrate. I remember Nicholas, on seeing a red-tinted sunset, running around excitedly shouting, 'Rudolf the Red-Nosed Reindeer is coming!' I borrowed rituals from my childhood in Poland. We laid out cookies and milk next to the fireplace for Father Christmas. We rang bells from the terrace so that the children thought he was on his way. The next morning, we sprinkled powdered sugar over Simon's shoes to create the outlines of footsteps next to the Christmas tree overloaded with presents. Once we started travelling, we began a collection of Christmas ornaments. Wherever we went, the challenge was to find a bauble most representative of the country we were visiting. We have a large collection that now hangs on our very eclectic tree every year.

I don't think we are traditional parents. We have always believed in broadening our sons' horizons as much as possible and telling them the truth from early on. Religion can be a tricky subject to navigate when you have young children. While Simon was an indifferent Anglican, I grew up strictly Roman Catholic, a religion I abandoned when I left Poland. I believed all the dogma instilled in me, but I was a voracious reader. When I arrived in South Africa, I signed up to a library and took a weekly bus to the middle of town to exchange one pile of books for another. One of the books I read was Michael Baigent and Richard Leigh's *The Holy Blood and the Holy Grail*. For the first time, I learnt that Jesus Christ was an actual man who lived, worked and possibly even married. I was thirteen and remember being shocked. I had been taught not to question religion. Questions were inconvenient. Consequently, I wanted my children to understand all religions. And so we built exposure to different religions into our travels. India turned out to be the best place to do that. We wanted to make sure that when they grew up, they could make up their own minds about what they wanted to believe, or not believe. More importantly, we wanted them to grow up with a strong set of values and morals.

On a lighter note, we did see a Jesus Christ lizard run on water in Costa Rica. It was on that same trip that I tried to impart the value of hard work to the boys. While on a hiking trail in a tropical rainforest, we encountered a crossroads. One of the signs was marked as a shortcut. The boys immediately opted to go that way, but I turned to them and told them that there are no shortcuts in life. We went the long way.

Another sensitive topic is sex education. We made our first attempt when the boys were eleven and nine. We decided that as an opener to the awkward discussion we would walk with them through the red-light district of Amsterdam, exposing them to all its 'tourist attractions'. Mind you, by that stage the red-light district had become relatively mild and we undertook our expedition during the daytime. Unfortunately, they were so engrossed in discussing Greek myths that they didn't even look up, let alone ask any questions. It was a disappointing failure, which led to Simon eventually having 'the talk' with two very bored teenagers.

As I've mentioned, one of the most important skills I've learnt is to use my voice. It's a skill that I have passed on to my children. When they were about ten, I hired an acting coach to teach them to act and project their voices. Every week, Alex and Nicholas had one-on-one sessions. This served them well in the years to come, when at school they joined the public-speaking and debating society and won numerous awards in South Africa and internationally. When Alex was selected to represent South Africa in the 2015 World Individual Debating and Public Speaking Championships in Hong Kong, we had no idea what to expect. We decided to travel with him and support him. Without our knowledge or input, he delivered a speech on the life-threatening trials and tribulations that refugees go through to obtain asylum. He used me as an example, and had everyone in tears. He went on to represent South Africa again in 2016 in Pittsburgh in the United States, while Nicholas took over the baton in 2017 in Sydney, Australia, and in 2018 in Cape Town. Given that the South African team averaged around ten students, having a son on the team in each of these years was quite an achievement.

The acting lessons and the prizes they won subsequently helped both my sons get into prestigious Ivy League universities in the United States. I would encourage every parent to send their child to similar lessons, societies and clubs. The ability to speak and articulate thoughts confidently will serve them well as their careers unfold.

We are extremely proud of our sons. They are similar in some ways, different in others. They've never competed. They never take anything for granted. They worked hard at school to achieve academic success. Everything they have done has been based on merit. They have a different surname to me, and most people don't even know that I'm their mother. They aren't flashy and never disclose the fact that they are wealthy, or that they have travelled as extensively as they have. For Nicholas's twenty-first, I put together a collage of our travels. Most of his friends were surprised. Both boys have chosen their friends carefully – academically gifted, kind-hearted and principled young people who are neither particularly wealthy nor wild.

Alex is the literary one in the family, and he has written many essays and poems over the years. When he was nine, every boy in his class was given the task of delivering a well-known poem at a school performance. Alex asked if he could perform one of his own poems. He was a huge fan of *The Lord of the Rings* and his poem, called 'Sword Slash', had a refrain along the lines of:

> *Sword Slash!*
> *Fight back the orcs!*
> *Sword Slash!*
> *Go call the hawks!*

It was quite a feat and everyone cheered. But he thought his peers made fun of him after that. Years later, he went river-rafting with some of the older boys from school and was asked to recite the poem. It was then that he realised he'd become a bit of a legend. It was an indescribable boost to his self-confidence and he even made it the topic of his admission essay to Columbia University in New York. I was sad in a way when he gave up writing to study computer science. He has taken up another hobby, however, as seriously as he does everything else. He loves cooking and has taken professional classes to ensure he can entertain his friends and family in style.

Nicholas is a collector. In high school he made a point of being awarded every school colour and tie, from academics and debating to drama, public relations and even rock climbing. He is also an amazing performer and a talented singer. He has a deep operatic bass singing voice and was a member of the school's a cappella group. Despite studying hardcore subjects as part of his PPE degree at the University of Pennsylvania, as part of an initial plan to become a human rights lawyer, he dreams of being a stage actor. He wants to go to acting school in the UK after he finishes his undergraduate degree. Now that I have time to be a supportive mother, I travel to the US to watch him perform. He is a kind, old soul. If there is a person in need, be it a child crying or a woman carrying heavy bags, he is the first to rush to help. His small but continuous acts of kindness towards strangers always catch us by surprise. He is also the one who looks after me and phones me regularly to check if I'm okay.

Alex has a great sense of humour. His comic, off-the-cuff chirps have kept us entertained for years. Nicholas, for his part, is the date-keeper in the family; he remembers the dates of every trip we have ever taken. 'Yes, he is a date-keeper,' Alex chirped recently. 'He keeps all his dates in the basement.' Nicholas, to our great annoyance, also loves to keep secrets from us. When we travelled to Japan on a family holiday, he amazed us by speaking Japanese to the cab driver who collected us from the airport. Apparently, he had learnt the language by watching anime on the internet. He had also familiarised himself with Japanese culture and history ahead of the trip and became a useful 'guide', particularly when we stumbled on a shop selling my much-coveted Monchhichi dolls. For years we had no idea that he'd joined the school choir. And in his final year, when he was selected to become a member of the Ten Club, the school's most prestigious club, I only found out when I started receiving congratulatory WhatsApps from the other parents.

Despite their differences, Alex and Nicholas are best friends. I always tell them that when the going gets tough, as it invariably does, the one thing they can depend on is each other.

I've already mentioned something about our travels, which has been another of our great advantages as a family. Every school holiday, we took our sons on whirlwind trips overseas. From Antarctica and the Arctic to Cambodia, India, Galapagos and Vietnam, there is not a corner of the world we have not explored. In this way, we were able to spend short yet concentrated periods of time together. Nothing bonds a family like a dip in the Antarctic Ocean on a dare, eating worms in Mexico and sitting on the ruins of Machu Picchu discussing ancient history.

By exposing our sons to different cultures, religions, locations and languages, we gave them a solid foundation and expanded their knowledge base. I believe those trips were an integral part of their early education. The world is changing rapidly and history is disappearing. On our first visit to Vietnam, Saigon was full of craft shops and street vendors. Three years later, they had been replaced by shopping malls. It is important to keep documenting the past, as we cannot rely on survivors and oral history forever. To this day, when Alex and Nicholas are together, they debate and discuss what they learnt on their travels. Where India was an education in religion, the Galápagos Islands allowed them to follow in the footsteps of Darwin, and Antarctica and the Arctic exposed them to the effects of climate change. There is nothing more powerful than standing in front of melting glaciers to understand its impact.

Wherever we travel, we try to meet locals who can explain the history and the politics of the country to us. In Myanmar, we met Aung San Suu Kyi's personal assistant, who lived and worked alongside the politician while she was imprisoned by the military. She explained Aung San Suu Kyi the person as opposed to the public figure, her father's role in Burmese independence, her military background and her lifelong quest for acceptance by the very regime that imprisoned her. Ever since that visit, nothing Suu Kyi has done on the political stage has come as a surprise. When, as state counsellor, she defended the Burmese military against allegations of genocide against the Rohingya people before the International Court of Justice, I could trace her actions back to what we were told by her assistant. We were in Myanmar when the genocide was at its peak. No one was permitted to talk about it, there was very little information available other than satellite images of burning villages, and even our English guide was reluctant to explain what was happening on the ground.

Chance encounters with locals often leave us with invaluable wisdom. On a trip to Mexico, we asked our Mexican driver about his American accent. He told us that he had spent several years working in the United States, earning a good living, but he was miserable. The work was hard and took him away from home. Although the money was good, he never got to enjoy it. He decided to return home to Mexico, to a tiny village on the coast. While he earns very little, he said, it is enough if he budgets carefully. More importantly, he told us, he leads a happy life. Given that we spend most of our lives at work, we need to like the work and the people we work with, so we can come home every day with a smile on our face.

We also like to use local guides. They usually provide a lot more colour to what we see and experience and are a wealth of information on the history and culture of each region. In Cambodia, our guide had been a child when Pol Pot and the Khmer Rouge seized power in 1975 and embarked on the Cambodian genocide, in which nearly a quarter of the country's population was murdered. Listening to his story was a reminder that democracy and respect for human rights are luxuries afforded to few.

Meeting people from all walks of life has taught me to look at all facets of an issue or problem. My views and opinions are never set in stone – a lesson I learnt in childhood, having experienced the realities of communism in Poland and then seeing the perceptions about it outside the country. Listening to a North Vietnamese soldier's take on the war in Vietnam offers a very different perspective to the Hollywood version most of us grew up with. Based on such experiences, I have learnt to form my opinions based on interactions with many people with differing viewpoints. This has served me well in the boardroom. Respected leaders are those who have an open mind and can see matters from the perspective of a multitude of cultures.

Although the internet provides a window onto the world that many believe renders travel unnecessary, it is not a substitute for real-life experiences, for actually interacting with people of different cultures and for learning to problem-solve on the spot. I have drawn many lessons from our travels that I have since translated and absorbed into my working life. Understanding different economies, policies and cultures helps one to think more globally. Global thinking is an essential skill for any business leader, as it is key to making sound business and investment decisions, domestically and internationally. Travelling the world, even for short periods of time with your family, is a valuable way to gain this skill.

I think another key to my success both at home and in the workplace is my approach to health. Life is full of stressors. Given my past, I suffer from regular anxiety attacks. So do many women I have met on my journey, particularly those working in the financial services industry. Good health is a privilege. For women, however, that privilege is often denied due to the pressures placed on them at work and at home. It all takes a toll. Anxiety attacks, thyroid issues, insomnia, rheumatoid arthritis, migraines and many other immunological diseases, all often attributed to stress, affect more women than men.

Many women do not talk about their health, particularly in the workplace where being strong and 'as good as a man' means that any show of weakness is stigmatised. I have a different approach. I have never been afraid to talk about my medical issues, a lot of which I attribute to stress. Besides anxiety, I also have reading epilepsy. So what? It doesn't make me any less capable. I find that sharing my issues with staff and friends often leads to other women coming forward and talking to me about their own medical conditions. I am fortunate in that I can afford the best care, so I always try to point them in the right direction.

During my second pregnancy, while still working at Coronation, I developed rheumatoid arthritis, an immunological disease associated with stress. Running on an uneven road was not an option, so I turned to the treadmill. Two hours every morning. It is a healthy way of producing enough endorphins to get me through the day. Simon hates the fact that wherever we go in the world, I require a treadmill. In Myanmar in 2017, we took a riverboat on the Irrawaddy River. I was assured there would be a treadmill on board. Of course, when we went to meet the boat in a small rural village in the middle of nowhere, there was no treadmill. We were accompanied by our guide, Max, who was highly knowledgeable about the country. With one of the poorest economies in the world, arriving in Myanmar is like stepping into the past. Farmers and fishermen trade their goods, there are few paved roads and the many different tribes are united by a military junta protecting its lucrative heroin trade. Max was a fun guy who came from a well-known English family. He called himself a 'villa filler'. When he learnt of the missing treadmill, Max sprang into action. Two hours later, we watched in disbelief as four men carried a working treadmill onboard. Where Max located that treadmill, I will never know. As an aside, food poisoning in Myanmar is a known danger. I was ultra-cautious throughout our visit and congratulated myself on our last day in the country for having escaped the scourge. Perhaps unsurprisingly, I was flown out of Myanmar semi-conscious in a wheelchair after eating sushi in a smart restaurant before departure.

I also cycled in my youth and have about six Argus Cycle Tours under my belt. Training involved waking up at five o'clock in the morning every Sunday in the weeks leading up to the race. My best time was about four hours. During one tour, after conquering the notoriously difficult Suikerbossie hill, another cyclist bumped into me and his handlebars hooked into mine. He managed to stay upright and cycled on, but I fell. Some kind people helped me up and pushed me on my way. Thankfully, it was downhill all the way to the end. When I crossed the finish line, I must have looked a sight, because the medics immediately pulled me into the emergency tent. I had a broken elbow and blood was streaming down my leg.

I have a high pain tolerance, although that's not necessarily a good thing. While skiing a few years ago, I had a mild fall. My shoulder hurt, but we had a few more days of skiing ahead of us and I was reluctant to cut the trip short. A few painkillers and a compress made of packed snow helped me to continue. When I returned to South Africa, it turned out I had broken my shoulder and torn all the ligaments. I had to have two operations. My friends joke that they still remember me running on a treadmill with my arm in a sling.

I eat fairly healthily, and I am a vegetarian by choice. As a university student, when I announced that I no longer ate meat, my grandmother kept preparing veal, trying to persuade me that it was a vegetable. Coming from a relatively 'rotund' family, and with a mixed Jewish and Polish heritage – where food, particularly bread, potatoes and cakes, is key to socialising – I have to watch what I eat. I struggled with my weight in my teenage years. I recently met an old friend from university who hadn't seen me for twenty-five years. The first words out of his mouth? 'You were a lot rounder when I last saw you!' I have never been a believer in restricting foods for the sake of weight loss. In my experience, diets do not work in the long term. I rather watch what I eat, I never deny myself a piece of cake, and I follow an interim-fasting approach. I seldom have breakfast. I then have either lunch or dinner, never both. I snack on fruit and nuts in between. This has served me well over the years.

Besides the stresses of work and home, women have the added pressure of having to look a certain way. Looking professional matters, irrespective of sex or gender and the position you hold. For women, however, the bar is even higher. I am a strong opponent of what I now see on social media, where women feel the need to use Photoshop and filters to completely distort their natural looks. It is a crazy and unrealistic approach to beauty, and it places further pressure on young women, and women pursuing careers in particular, to alter their appearance. Girls as young as fifteen now have lip fillers, fake eyelashes and hair extensions. Behind each of these girls are parents who are enabling massive insecurity among those who do not measure up. I am reminded of the lessons my father determinedly ingrained in us: never rely on a man and never get into a position where you're washing some man's underwear; what other people think of you is irrelevant; and be confident in yourself and your decision-making.

10

African Harvest

M Y RESIGNATION FROM CORONATION, effective 1 April 2003, was regarded by many as an April Fool's joke. But it was no joke to me. I had spent six and a half years overseeing Coronation's growth from a start-up to one of the premier investment management companies in South Africa. I was instrumental to that growth and to the early strategy of the company. Internally, I was party to every decision and responsible for far too many functions. In fact, in many cases, I performed the function. For many clients, I was the face of Coronation. I was its marketing, business development, product development, legal and client servicing divisions. Externally, and despite my age, I was taken seriously in every boardroom in South Africa as I gathered clients one by one. I never envisaged leaving Coronation at a stage when growth could only have been exponential and when I was one of the four most senior people in the business. I certainly did not foresee leaving the company on the terms that I did.

Adrenaline and panic drove me for the next six months. It did not help that the CEO of Coronation dogged my every step and publicly blamed me for everything that went wrong after I left. He learnt the hard way that letting someone walk out the door is easy; replacing their knowledge is not. Several of the people appointed to positions I had held were inexperienced, with little institutional knowledge. It was easy, and career enhancing, to sing from the same hymn sheet as the boss. They subsequently started losing clients.

The restraint-of-trade clause meant I could not immediately look for another job in the financial services industry. I consulted a lawyer about the validity of an agreement signed under emotional duress, but he gave me a valuable piece of advice: never sue anyone with deeper pockets than you. So, the day after I resigned, I dragged Simon to the accounting offices of a friend to ask about setting up our own business, as well as a family trust. The next day, we registered our first company, IQvest. Our family trust was registered on 3 May 2003, with seed capital of R1 000.

I could have waited out the six months and then started to look for another position, but after my experience at Coronation, I was determined to never again work for a man, or 'wash his underwear', as my father would say.

We rented premises and used our mortgage bond to decorate it. Interior design is a bit of a passion of mine, and the decor immediately gave our small office space a feeling of being in business. Using the knowledge I had gleaned from my time at Alexander Forbes, and Simon's consulting skills, IQvest provided investment advisory services to retirement funds. We were joined by my loyal team of two, quantitative genius Willem van der Merwe and my assistant, Ronel Bantjes, who had both followed me out of Coronation saying that they did not need salaries until such time as I could afford to pay them. As flattering as this may seem, it put even more pressure on me to make a success of this business. Some of our former colleagues helped set up the office and IT infrastructure as a favour, risking their jobs and working after hours in secret. Everything had to be done quietly, as we were petrified of breaching my termination agreement. In fact, the new receptionist we hired somehow found out about our fears and blackmailed us for a significant sum of money. I was sufficiently inexperienced to pay up.

As our office and small team took shape, I began to realise that there were many aspects of running my own business I had yet to learn. One harsh lesson I learnt early on was that, as much as your clients love you, they love the brand behind you more. None of the clients I secured for Coronation contacted me or were willing to follow me. My personal low came when, after taking the cheapest flight to Johannesburg, I rented the cheapest car from a no-frills budget rental company located at the far end of a long corridor of more prestigious rental agencies. Every cent mattered, but every step away from Avis and Hertz towards the 'no-name brand' rental agency felt like a step down the ladder of success. After fifteen minutes of searching the parking area for the tiny car I had just rented, I put down the heavy bags I was carrying and burst into tears.

I also learnt that when you start a business, you are approached by a lot of shady characters who want to 'leverage' you by collaborating. In those early days, our small boardroom hosted a stream of such people and their unsavoury ideas. I will never forget one individual who had recently resigned from a company being investigated for fraud. He approached us to explain how the fraud had been perpetrated and to offer to help us do the same! Having said that, we also encountered some successful and generous people who believed in us and offered genuine help.

As time went by, we acquired enough clients to start paying small salaries to our ragtag team, which by then had grown to include Iain Anderson, who heads up my investment team today, and a brilliant computer software developer, Joseph Potgieter. Our clients wanted more than just advice on how to invest their money, though. They wanted us to actively manage their 'selection' of appointed investment managers. Consequently, we pivoted our business model from consulting to offering products based on our selection of who we considered to be the best managers in their field. Flexibility is key to starting a business, particularly in the initial phases.

Many people believe that investment management involves a blend of art and science, and that alchemy happens in the lofty offices of those fund managers who make millions and drive fancy sports cars. Nothing could be further from the truth. A day in the life of an average fund manager is fairly mundane. On arrival at the office, normally around 9 a.m., the morning meeting is held, during which a junior trader does a quick summary of what happened in the markets the day before and possibly overnight. Some listen, while others read the newspapers. After the meeting and some chit-chat, everyone goes back to their desks. Junior analysts, who are allocated a limited number of companies to analyse, open spreadsheets and stare at the same financials of the same companies as they did the day before, and the day before that, perhaps tweaking their forecasts by inserting some new data into the models. They might update research reports for the fund managers to review or give a quick presentation.

Fund managers themselves do not have to build financial models. They pull up software on their computer screens that shows the performance of individual stocks on the day, and they open newsfeeds from companies such as Bloomberg and Reuters. Most of the time, they read. The day is usually broken by a trip to the gym at lunchtime, or the odd visit from a company's management team to explain their financial results. Regular meetings are held to discuss the economy, individual companies, politics and the weather. Based on those meetings, a decision may be made to buy or sell shares in a company. In some companies, individual fund managers are allowed flexibility to manage their own funds, in others all decisions are made collectively. Almost no one works past 5 p.m.

The most active time for an investment management company is bonus time, when individual performance is evaluated and real money is allocated. Not much has changed since my Coronation days. At least a month before, the whispers and plotting start. Because the pool is finite, everyone wants to maximise their share, which is only possible at the expense of others. Consequently, all real collaboration ceases. If there is a formula for splitting the bonus, a lot of energy is expended on thinking of ways to skew the formula in one's favour. But at the end of the day, each fund manager carries an invisible gun: 'Pay me X or I walk out.' A lot of money is spent on promoting the individual fund managers as the brightest in the industry, and so no investment management company wants a walk-out. The game is therefore rigged from the start. The investment team always wins. The company always loses. Bonus day is usually punctuated with the slamming of doors, raised voices and occasional tears. Then the cycle starts again.

Disillusioned with the performance of 'active' managers, I revived my love affair with index tracking. As I have described, instead of divining the future value of any one company and investing in who you think will be the 'winner', you buy all the shares listed on the stock market in the same proportion as they are represented in a recognised 'market index' published by the stock exchange and used to measure the performance of the whole market. Not only do you do less, but you can also charge less.

At IQvest, we decided that if we were to offer products, we needed software to administer our clients' accounts. Buying anything off the shelf was prohibitively expensive, and so Joseph, our software development genius, began to pay his way by writing the initial code of what became the skeleton for all our future business ventures. He wrote code as easily as Mozart composed music. We were extremely fortunate to have him.

As the days passed and the financial stresses increased, I received a lunch invitation from an old friend from my Southern Life days. As I wound my way between the tables towards my friend waving at me from the back of the restaurant, I realised that he was not alone. Sitting across from him was a jovial-looking man who I recognised but could not immediately place. When I reached the table, he stuck out his hand and said, 'Hi, I am Mzi Khumalo. I believe you have a business. I have a business. Let's make a deal.'

Now, I had fancy offices, but I knew I didn't really have a business. What I did not know was that neither did he. Mzi had purchased an investment management company called African Harvest from the very same shareholders that owned Coronation. Unfortunately, it was the antithesis of Coronation in terms of success – an embarrassing financial failure with poor management and little market recognition. In fact, when Mzi came along, the company was in the process of being wound up. I knew none of this at the time. We hammered out the details in a frenzy over lunch, negotiating relative shareholdings, timelines and a new structure. African Harvest would 'buy' our shareholding in IQvest for shares in African Harvest, all IQvest staff would move across to African Harvest and I would become CEO of the combined entity. Mzi insisted that I sign the agreements that weekend. When I got back to the office, I called everyone together and, to their bemusement, announced that I had sold IQvest. I am not sure who was more shocked: my staff, my husband or me.

At the time, Mzi Khumalo was a controversial figure in the South African business community. He was one of ten siblings, his father had died when he was a young boy and he was raised by his mother and grandfather in KwaMashu township, outside Durban. Mzi's grandfather ruled the violent township with an iron fist. 'No one ever crossed my grandfather twice,' he once told me. Although an entrepreneur at heart, Mzi joined Umkhonto we Sizwe in the 1970s. In 1978 he was arrested, charged with treason and sentenced to twenty years on Robben Island. He ended up spending twelve years in prison alongside the giants of the struggle, including Nelson Mandela, Walter Sisulu, Govan Mbeki and Ahmed Kathrada. While there, he studied for a Bachelor of Commerce degree by correspondence and acted as a referee in soccer matches because, apparently, no one dared cross him either.

After a short stint in politics upon his release, Mzi went into business determined to make money. To this end, he concluded one of the first black economic empowerment (BEE) deals in South Africa, becoming a shareholder in a gold-mining company. He then took advantage of a loophole in the agreement and, with some complex corporate structuring, sold the shares and became an instant billionaire. Controversy swirled about how he had bought out minorities in the deal and then shifted some of the proceeds overseas, out of the reach of the South African Reserve Bank. Mzi became an overnight business sensation, but also a target for anyone with a dodgy plan or deal. His weakness was a reliance on verbal agreements. He would sign legal documents without reading them, basing his decisions on trust and a handshake. This exposed him to exploitation. Whenever he discovered that he had been cheated, he would renege on the agreement, and negative publicity, court cases and criticism would inevitably follow. While he is often referred to as 'controversial', his personal dealings with me were always honourable. I eventually got used to the frequent phone calls from Mzi prefaced with, 'Magda, brace yourself for tomorrow's headlines.'

I took over running African Harvest on 1 October 2003. My time there was gruelling. It really was a complete corporate mess heading for liquidation. Like me when I left Coronation, Mzi had not read what he signed. He consequently inherited all the liabilities associated with the company, including its many tussles with the tax authorities.

The first hint that everything was not well was when I arrived at the African Harvest offices for my first day of work. The reception was dark and gloomy, and there was a hole in the wall behind the receptionist's desk. I looked up to see that half the lightbulbs in the overhead lights were burnt out. When I asked the receptionist about the hole in the wall, she told me it had been there for a while because there was no one to fix it. That turned out to be the case for the entire company. She showed me to my small, sparsely furnished office. A large white envelope lay on the desk. Apprehensively, I opened it to find a bulky due diligence report that Mzi had commissioned after buying the company. Usually, these reports are requested prior to signing any agreement, but, as was his way, Mzi had bought African Harvest on trust.

The due diligence report detailed a litany of horrors, from staff and tax issues to blatant financial mismanagement. I immediately phoned Mzi to ask what on earth I was dealing with. I will never forget his response. 'Magda,' he said, 'it is not that I did not tell you the truth. It is just that you really did not ask the right questions.' He was right, of course. Blinded by the prospects of building a business without the stress of having no revenue, I hadn't asked anything. Had I known the Herculean task I was taking on, I certainly would have negotiated a higher stake in the company.

The next revelation explained the speed with which I was expected to sign the agreements. African Harvest had an existing CEO, a clever investment professional with some personal issues. His party trick when under the influence of alcohol was to strip in front of crowds. This did not go down well with Mzi. The weekend I signed my contract of employment and shareholder agreements, Mzi summoned the CEO to Johannesburg to tell him that he was being replaced. Mzi fully expected him to resign, but he did not. Instead, he returned to Cape Town and announced to the staff that they should just ignore me as he would 'finish me off' in a couple of months. Needless to say, he didn't succeed and was himself gone within a few months. He was followed by the CFO, who had refused to give me access to the management accounts.

I believe that to run a successful company you need to incentivise key staff. I learnt the lesson of being a 'shareholder with no shares' at Coronation and was determined not to make the same mistakes. The first step was to negotiate an actual shareholding in African Harvest for the investment team and senior staff. This was no easy feat, as Mzi clearly felt he'd overpaid for the company and was no pushover when it came to negotiations. Eventually, however, I succeeded in ensuring that everyone was pulling in the same direction.

There were many rocky moments in those early days, but there were some humorous ones too. A few months after I took over as CEO, I heard angry voices outside my office. On enquiry, I learnt that the investment team had just found out my age from a newspaper article. Apparently, everyone thought I was forty. I guess it was bad enough being managed by a woman, but worse still to discover she was only thirty-two.

Mzi provided plenty of colour to my days at African Harvest. He referred to Nelson Mandela as 'the old man' and told me stories that reminded me that our beloved former president was as human as the rest of us. Mzi drove a flashy Bentley sports car. One evening when I met him for dinner in Durban, he took me for a spin to show off KwaMashu. As the luxury car joggled along the uneven roads into the heart of the township, I was convinced we were heading for certain death. Mzi laughed away my fears. No one would touch him, he said. He was right. Instead, people came out of their shacks and waved.

Mzi enjoyed his money. Early on he told me that if he died, he didn't want to be buried with it – he would spend it while he could. Coming from someone who had survived what he had, it made sense. For a man who has faced torture and death in prison, he retains a great sense of humour.

One of the more surreal experiences involving Mzi occurred in August 2004, when he rented the *Christina O* – the superyacht once owned by billionaire Greek shipowner Aristotle Onassis and famous for its bar-stools upholstered in whale foreskin – for the duration of the Olympic Games in Greece. *Christina O* is known for having hosted people such as Winston Churchill, the Kennedys, Maria Callas, Rainier III, Prince of Monaco, Grace Kelly, Marilyn Monroe, Frank Sinatra and many others. Mzi laughed when he explained that he'd had problems paying for the rental as the Reserve Bank did not believe the size of the invoice he pre-sented. The plan was to host then president Thabo Mbeki and his entire cabinet on board the yacht. Mzi and Mbeki had been friends for years and apparently had some kind of bet on the experience. Simon and I flew to Crete in a private jet, a first for me, and boarded the *Christina O*. We were the only non-ANC-affiliated couple and I'm sure we looked like pale fish out of water.

Unfortunately, a few days before all the politicians were due to arrive, a Sunday newspaper got hold of the story and Mbeki decided to cancel. As a result, Mzi and his wife, Khosi, his financial director Andile Reve and his wife, and Simon and I were the only passengers on the most famous yacht in Greece. Wherever we went, we were followed by other yachts and ships with people constantly taking photographs. The yacht had a crew complement of forty, was outrageously opulent and completely at our disposal. There were five chefs on board and Mzi would set them cooking challenges every evening.

The *Christina O* also came with an invitation to the best seats at both the opening and closing ceremonies of the Olympic Games. In between, we sailed – to Bodrum, Turkey, where we were VIP guests at an elegant nightclub; to the Greek island of Santorini, where we rode donkeys up to its capital city, Fira; and to the volcanic island of Stromboli, off the coast of Sicily. When we arrived in Sicily, we docked in the harbour and a large crowd of people gathered, ready to photograph whatever celebrities were on board. Their disappointment was palpable as we walked down the gangway. Luckily, Khosi is an incredibly beautiful woman, so I'm sure at least some of the onlookers thought she was famous, even if they couldn't name her. My lasting memory of the *Christina O* experience is Mzi, sitting at the dining room table with a Renoir painting in the background, paraphrasing Honoré de Balzac with a smile on his face, 'Magda, behind every great fortune there is always a small crime.'

That same year, I was nominated by KPMG for the 2004 Business Leader of the Year award. It was a token nomination – they had to have at least one woman in the line-up. I had not done anything yet to deserve it. Fortunately, I did not win, but I did get to meet Pam Golding, the doyenne of real estate in South Africa and the first self-made woman I had ever met. She was seated at our table, and talking to her was hugely inspiring.

I always describe my three years at African Harvest as my 'swan years'. On the surface we were calm and collected, marketing African Harvest as the best investment manager in the country. Underneath, however, we were paddling frantically to steady the ship and keep it going. And we succeeded, for a while. A big part of the credit must go to my CFO, Niki Giles, who embraced virtually any challenge thrown her way.

While I was struggling with African Harvest, Coronation was experiencing its own turbulence. Most of the investment team gradually resigned, resulting in a near-collapse of the business. It was salvaged at the last minute, but the infamous CEO departed shortly thereafter. I observed it all from my corner office, which, as fate would have it, overlooked Coronation's building.

African Harvest was my mini-MBA. I had to learn all the aspects of running a business where you are responsible for all the decision-making, from the 'toilet paper' issues, such as what carpets to put down in the newly redecorated office space, to the 'macro' issues, such as financial budgeting and managing unruly staff.

Slowly we persuaded retirement funds to trust us with their assets. But as the assets and thus the bonus pool grew, so did the discontent and greed. It was Coronation all over again. The bonus negotiations were a continual headache. It is almost impossible to hold anyone to account for investment performance when they're holding the invisible gun. I remember one prominent member of the investment team telling me that he deserved all the additional shares I was allocating because 'in life, you have to look after number one'. In many ways, this summed up the lot of them.

Money brings out the worst in people. I have made my money through a combination of hard work, skills I picked up in my youth, being in the right place at the right time with the right idea, and a healthy dose of luck. I have never fought for money or betrayed others to get it. I have certainly never reached the point of being willing to do anything for money. Unfortunately, the same cannot be said about many successful people in the investment management industry. The bigger the organisation, the more an individual's success depends on the failure of others. Someone once aptly described it as setting people up for failure and dancing on their graves. One thing is certain, the saddest people I have met are those whose only achievement in life is having made a lot of money. Their wealth is their sole validation. Validation matters. Money certainly helps, but on its own, it is meaningless.

Eventually, the 'pay us more or we leave' got tiring, particularly for Mzi, who calculated that given the growth of African Harvest he could sell the company and recover his initial investment. He called me one day in March 2006, completely out of the blue, and told me to sell the company within two weeks.

11

The Art of the Deal

GIVEN THAT AFRICAN HARVEST WAS slowly starting to feel like a mini Coronation, I wasn't sorry to let it go. On Mzi's instructions, I embarked on yet another crash course in my home-styled MBA. Borrowing a phrase from Donald Trump, I had to quickly learn 'the art of the deal'. Mzi gave me barely any guidance, and the only 'corporate advisors' on the scene were his bankers, who needed the deal to happen to claim their share of the proceeds as repayment for a loan Mzi had taken out. They spent their time pressurising me to conclude the transaction at all costs and as quickly as possible. As soon as I figured out their motives, I threw them out. They reappeared on the day we signed the sale agreement to claim the loan repayment.

A few competitors expressed interest, including a party brought to the table by the investment team, who were promised various incentives to tilt the deal in their favour. It was a stressful time, but one in which I learnt a lot.

We eventually narrowed down the bidders to two: a financial services group with no investment management interests who wanted to broaden their financial footprint, and the African Harvest investment team's collaborators. The financial services group performed a detailed due diligence on every aspect of the company, from its staff and finances to its legal agreements, and so on. They even visited the largest clients to ensure they had their support for the transaction. The collaborators did none of that, relying entirely on the assurances they received from the investment team. I was sufficiently worried about this approach to request a meeting with them to try to persuade them to perform their own due diligence. I flew to Johannesburg where I met with yet another bunch of white males who dismissed me on the spot.

Eventually we reached the end of the line, with the two tenders arriving five minutes apart. The timing was critical, as it appeared that the collaborators had waited to hear what the financial services group bid before putting in their final offer, which was marginally higher. It emerged that they were getting inside information from someone in Mzi's office who hoped to be appointed to a senior position in the new company. Shortly after the tenders arrived, I received an angry phone call from Mzi, who had uncovered the 'spy' within his ranks at the last minute. He instructed me not to sell to the collaborators under any circumstances. I was not about to disagree, particularly as they had done no due diligence on the company or its clients. The outcry from the investment team was so intense that an industrial psychologist had to be brought in to calm them down. Adults behaving like spoilt children is not uncommon in the investment management industry. Many of them earn way too much money too early on and never gain the maturity that comes with struggling to achieve success.

So we accepted the financial services group's offer, but this turned out to be the beginning rather than the end of the drama of negotiating a corporate transaction. The next three months were a real eye-opener. Selling a business is never simple. It involves hashing out multiple legal agreements, complex nuanced clauses, and indemnities for every eventuality. To put it into perspective, our final set of agreements when printed was over eleven centimetres thick.

The group that bought African Harvest, Cadiz Holdings, despite being a JSE-listed company, was more of a rugby club than anything else. All male, they could not come to terms with the fact that they had to negotiate with a young woman. The CEO had recently attended a course at the University of Pennsylvania's Wharton School of Business and boasted that he would deploy his newly acquired skills of 'negotiating by exhaustion'. In his interpretation, this meant negotiating through the night, rather than during the day, and bringing in a tag-team so that I had to negotiate with fresh individuals while I was exhausted. Another tactic, as I was subsequently told, was to scare off the senior corporate lawyer I employed to help with the transaction by threatening to never use his firm in future if he advised me through the negotiations. The lawyer, obviously cowed, sent his junior legal assistant, who actually turned out to be brilliant. Allan Hannie remains a true friend and someone I trust completely and use to this day.

When it comes to negotiating agreements, there are several strategies available to you. You can outsource everything to lawyers, negotiate through proxies, or engage in a battle of wills, bluffing and bullying. Cadiz chose the latter. Unfortunately for them, I had only one objective in mind: since they had offered R300 million for the business, they would pay R300 million. This is what I had promised Mzi. Having a clear goal in mind and being unwilling to compromise meant that I was not distracted by the 'noise' of the negotiations. My one piece of advice when entering any business transaction is to have a clear objective in mind from the start and from which you do not deviate. And never negotiate from a position of weakness, where you want the deal more than the other party. If you are in that position, rather walk away and look for an alternative.

The CEO's 'negotiating by exhaustion' ploy backfired early on. I have had insomnia since I was a child and switching from trying to sleep at night to doing so during the day wasn't too difficult. Tag-teaming also proved ineffectual, because often things were missed in the handovers. However, their attitude towards women was their real downfall. Here was a company whose culture openly classified women as ornamental rather than functional. The only way they knew how to negotiate with a woman was by showing aggression. A lot of aggression. They screamed and shouted and swore. Every clause on every page of the agreement was aggressively 'negotiated'. Here is where my junior lawyer came into his own. He could match them swearword for swearword. The more they screamed, the less coherent and detailed the negotiation became. I observed it all from my Perspex box of dissociation. At one stage, everyone was screaming so loudly that I simply left the boardroom. I called Mzi from the couch in reception and told him that I didn't think anyone had noticed that the person they were negotiating with had just left the room.

When I figured out that their main issue was negotiating with a woman, I decided to ramp up my feminine charm. My skirts became shorter, I tied my hair into a high ponytail and, for the first time in my life, I wore high-heeled boots that I bought specially for the occasion. It's ridiculous, but it enraged them and their attention to detail slipped even further. When negotiating, it's okay to look for your opponent's weak spots and exploit them. By triggering my opposition's rage, I managed to cloud their vision. Other situations may require a more empathetic approach as you try to convince people that you are really on their side.

It is also worthwhile to try to strike the preliminary deal without lawyers and corporate advisors in the room. Lawyers are predictable. In every instance, there comes a point when the lawyers meet behind their clients' backs to discuss a settlement amount that they think both parties may be pushed to agree to. Each then presents this to their respective client and pushes for a settlement. My advice is to take the lead and get in before the lawyers. Lawyers should only come in to ensure that all the agreements are watertight and that ultimately you 'read what you sign'.

After months of negotiation, we concluded a deal. The agreements were to be signed on a Friday night and announced to the market on Monday morning. Shareholders typically grant listed companies the right to conclude a deal within a prescribed timeframe, and if the date expires with no deal, new approvals need to be sought. The approvals for Cadiz expired at midnight on Saturday. It was their pumpkin hour. Because it was a weekend, they somehow thought they had the latitude to string me along and negotiate until Monday morning. It is apparently a common characteristic of all acquisitions that the offer is never what the purchaser actually intends to pay. I was about to learn this the hard way. As I was preparing that Friday to drive to Cadiz's offices to start signing the final agreements, I received a phone call from the CEO, who smugly told me that they were not prepared to pay the R300 million they initially offered and wanted a 'discount' of R30 million or else the transaction was off. I was taken aback and immediately phoned Mzi who said, perfectly calmly, that he was not going to be blackmailed.

The next morning, I went to a yoga class to calm my nerves and then to the hairdresser. In my mind, the deal was at the very least suspended. But the clock was ticking for Cadiz. Mid-Saturday afternoon, sitting in the hairdresser's chair, my wet hair wrapped up in a towel, my phone rang. It was the CEO, huffing and puffing and demanding to know why I was not at their offices to sign the papers. Everyone was waiting for me. There are few moments in life that you can savour for a lifetime. For me, this is one of them. I couldn't resist telling him that I was unavailable as I was having my hair done, but could perhaps pop by at five o'clock. I immediately called my lawyer, who was unfortunately unavailable, and so I went into the lion's den on my own. My first words as I walked into the boardroom were that if they did not immediately commit to paying R300 million I was walking out. This time they acceded, and we proceeded to checking all the documents one final time.

Even this simple matter turned into a circus. The lawyers advising the buyers were based in Johannesburg and all interaction to date had been conducted via video conferencing in the boardroom. This had not been a problem, until now. Out of the blue, the lawyers insisted that I could not be the only representative of African Harvest. They wanted someone else to countersign the agreements. Mzi was in Dubai, so we had to get Andile, Mzi's financial director who was based in Johannesburg, to join Cadiz's lawyers in their boardroom. Halfway through the evening, as we were going paragraph by paragraph through the agreements, the boardroom screen froze, but we could still hear them and so we continued.

At around eleven o'clock that night, we completed the checking and were ready to sign. As we took a roll call confirming everyone's agreement, a weak voice piped up from Johannesburg: 'Guys, Andile left at seven saying he's going to dinner and has not come back.' Chaos broke out as we realised that, despite his frozen smiling face on the screen before us, Andile was missing. I calmly phoned him and told him to get his butt back to the negotiating table. But he was having none of it. 'Magda, I haven't read through those agreements. If I sign what I shouldn't sign, Mzi will kill me.' I was livid. I had to wake up Mzi in Dubai and instruct him to send Andile back to the boardroom to start signing.

Even that did not go as planned. As the agreements had to be signed and countersigned both in Cape Town and Johannesburg, there was frantic faxing of required paperwork (in those days, faxing was still the most reliable way of instantly transferring documents). At some point, the fax machine in the lawyers' offices broke and Andile, accompanied by an entourage of lawyers and bankers, had to break a window at Mzi's offices across the road to access a working one. In a tumult of broken glass and blood, the deal was eventually signed and sealed. Relieved, we celebrated, taking photos and measuring the paperwork.

On Monday, I woke up to a public announcement that African Harvest had been sold. But all was not well. Not long after, a lawyer phoned me to say that, in our haste, we had missed one of the pages. This apparently rendered the entire agreement invalid, but it could be remedied by signing the page retrospectively, while preferably not making the issue public. Just as I was printing out the offending page, I received a call from someone who had overheard the Cadiz CEO bragging that, despite giving me his word, he still had absolutely no intention of paying R300 million for African Harvest. The agreement contained a loosely worded clause around tax indemnities and the ability of the buyer to withhold full payment in the event of suspected outstanding tax issues. There were no tax issues, as I had dealt with all of them during my tenure at African Harvest, a fact he was well aware of based on Cadiz's due diligence, but he seemingly planned to use that clause to withhold the final R30 million indefinitely.

I immediately phoned the CEO to tell him I would not sign the missing page until I had received a new, full and legally binding confirmation of payment. This led to another temper tantrum and another evening meeting, which involved a lot of pacing, rapid-fire monologue and at least one memorable quote, when he banged the table and told me he was not as stupid as he sounded. Perhaps not, but I got my R300 million and he got African Harvest. The bank involved in the transaction derisively named the deal their 'Mampara of the Year'.

The African Harvest I sold does not exist today other than as an extension of a private wealth manager, and the same is true of Cadiz

Holdings. Perhaps the leadership team, with its alpha-male culture, had something to do with their failure, but undoubtedly the majority of the blame can be placed on the investment team and their unreasonable demands. They have all since scattered, many to never work in the financial services industry again. I believe one of the senior members, the one who told me 'you have to look after number one', now breeds koi and other tropical fish for a living.

If I have one wish for the financial services industry it is that it would recognise the value of working collaboratively and remember that it is other people's money we have the privilege of managing. Every cent spent on a bonus comes from the pocket of a man or woman on the street. It is not a number. It is someone's livelihood. I guess it will be a long time before this mindset is embraced. Mzi recently asked me why I care if someone takes bribes or overcharges. I told him that encountering 'middlemen' is a fact of life in all industries, but where the middleman literally takes the money out of the pocket of someone who is saving for their retirement, that is a lack of morality I can never accept.

I always laugh at the fact that it took an ANC military commander to take a chance on a thirty-two-year-old blonde white woman. The white male-dominated financial services industry would not even give me a second glance, never mind a real chance. But Mzi did. In hindsight, I'm sure I wasn't his first choice. Frankly, I don't care. Taking over African Harvest, merging it with IQvest and turning it into the largest majority black-owned investment manager in the country provided the financial foundation for everything I have done since.

Mzi is a constant presence in my life. I still have long dinners with him, drinking fine wines and debating South African politics. He lives in London now, but nothing about him has changed. He was fairly amused at the thought of featuring in my book. We were dining at the best table in a posh gentlemen's club in London. We laughed at the fact that we stuck out like sore thumbs – he the only black man and me the only woman in the room. It reflected the financial services industry in which we first met.

12

A Woman in a Man's World

I AM OFTEN ASKED HOW I made it as 'a woman in a man's world'. The financial services industry is indeed a man's world, but I have never defined myself purely as a successful woman. My time at Southern Life taught me that women, like men, come in different colours, shapes and sizes. They have different motivations and approaches to their careers and priorities. My personal approach has always been one of working as hard as I can. I promote women and men equally and treat them the same. I do not look at people through the lens of gender, or any other lens for that matter. I look at the skills and talent they bring to the table. It is nevertheless an important question, and one that I will try to answer based on my personal experiences over the years, such as the fact that Coronation and African Harvest exposed me to the full extent of male domination in the world of finance.

Many women shun finance as a career. Apart from the aggressive culture of the industry, I think that many lack confidence when it comes to dealing with financial affairs. A 2018 survey conducted by Merrill Lynch showed that most women would rather talk about their own death than money. This has certainly been my experience. Women do not talk about money and many rely on husbands or partners to take care of their financial affairs. And this despite so many marriages ending in divorce, which almost always prejudices the woman financially. I remember one CEO asking me what monthly allowance he should pay his wife. An allowance is something you give a child, not a grown woman. Another fund manager asked me how I hid my money from Simon. He then proceeded to tell me how he hid his money from his wife in case they ever got divorced.

Unfortunately, when it comes to money, the odds are often stacked against women. We typically earn less than men for the same amount of work, we take time out of our jobs to raise children, setting our career progress back, and we spend more working hours doing unpaid labour such as housework. In South Africa, many women do not have formal employment and therefore have no retirement savings. Many also lack the means, awareness and skill to plan for the day when they are no longer able to work. Sadly, financial security and financial literacy are luxuries afforded to few.

I first became aware of the need to save for my retirement while working at Southern Life, where the concept of 'saving' was the lifeblood of the company. I had learnt the value of money early on, but never fully appreciated that the monthly cash flow would end when I was too old to work. At the same time, saving wasn't easy as I was expected to contribute a portion of my earnings to help my family. This is the norm in refugee families all around the world, as well as for many young black people in South Africa. With all this in mind, and despite the constraints, I taught myself to think of my salary as only ever being eighty per cent of what it really was. The other twenty per cent was deducted and invested in the company-sponsored retirement fund. I continued with this practice until I retired from formal employment. For most people, their retirement fund and their house make up their largest 'savings pot'. The most powerful tools when it comes to building wealth are discipline, thinking long term, and compound interest. Compound interest is how a small amount of money can grow exponentially over the long term as returns build on top of the initial investment as well as the returns already earned. To avoid temptation, I never looked at my investment or benefit statements. To me, that retirement fund did not exist. When I moved companies, the money was always transferred to the retirement fund offered by the new company. I have seen too many people access their retirement savings too early, consequently either retiring with much less than expected and having to trim down their standard of living, or not being able to retire when they wanted.

The best advice I can give anyone is to start saving from your very first pay cheque; put aside twenty per cent of your salary and do not think about that money again. Starting to save early makes sense. On average, assuming you start working at the age of twenty-five and retire at sixty-five, you will have roughly forty years to save. Most people these days live well into their nineties. That means that when you retire, that 'pot' must last you for the next thirty years – a time that unfortunately often involves significant medical bills. That is why so many elderly people today, having not prepared for the future when they were young, retire financially dependent on their children.

Many women are not as lucky as I was to be exposed to financial concepts early on. When it comes to building independent financial security, besides the tangible barriers such as pay inequality, glass ceilings and greater demands on our time, women face psychological barriers too. Our financial confidence is constantly being eroded by poorly conceived, often condescending financial messaging. Many targeted financial articles and adverts portray women as frivolous spenders who need to learn how to budget. With their focus on budgeting rather than saving, and with a tendency to scold rather than educate, these messages cement the notion that women and finance do not mix.

Financial literacy, never mind the direct knowledge gained by pursuing finance as a career, is another big barrier. Despite some progress, the world is not interested in specifically educating women about finance. It's up to women to educate other women. But there are so few women working in the financial services industry and being exposed to the more complex concepts of saving and investing that educators are few and far between. There is also a shortage of inspiring role models to emulate. Finance is not usually a topic of discussion at an average book club. If there were more women in finance, perhaps it would be. While more women are entering the workforce, starting businesses and saving, it's not happening fast enough. My early work experiences inspired me to take charge of my affairs. All I can hope is that my story inspires others to do the same.

Of course, none of this is helped by the fact that women have a much tougher time than men when it comes to general career progression, even before we can talk about hitting glass ceilings. Every professional woman I meet, no matter the industry, has a personal story about inequality in the workplace. And maybe this is partly how I managed to succeed in a man's world. Instead of trying to change this reality, I learnt to accept it, adapt to it and turn it to my advantage. But to win, I had to consciously step out of a traditional corporate. I too, despite my contribution and hard work, eventually hit a glass ceiling at Coronation.

Under communism, things were in some ways simpler, as everyone was equal. Women had the same opportunities as men, except in the mining sector. Incidentally, if women in the corporate arena think they have it hard, educate yourself about the plight of South Africa's female miners. Yes, they do exist. In the capitalist system, men have emerged as the clear economic winners, with supportive family structures having to form around their requirements. Without unity among women, and women taking control of their lives, this system will continue to perpetuate.

Women face many challenges in the workplace. We struggle to be taken seriously, and are often ignored and marginalised. I have learnt to survive by voicing my opinions passionately and ignoring my critics. It might make you unpopular in the short term, but it earns you respect. Work is not a popularity contest. You don't need to be liked by the people you manage, but you do need to be respected. That is what leadership is all about. Being everyone's best friend, or seeking their approval instead of giving constructive feedback, is counterproductive. We women are often our own worst enemies, particularly when we make it clear to our employers that we are not the primary breadwinner. This can make employers feel that we are not committed. You do not need to go to my extreme of not taking maternity leave and working through every weekend and holiday, but be sensible about the flexibility you demand.

I encourage young women to rely on their fathers for advice where possible. In an ideal world, fathers would recognise how difficult it is

Survivors of the Holocaust: my father, Adam, with his parents, Helunia and Gucio, in Gliwice, Poland, late 1940s.

A chubby three-year-old me.

On holiday in the Polish resort of Zakopane in the Tatra Mountains. Known for its skiing in the winter and hiking in the summer, it is also the cultural centre of the Górole, an ethnic group with its own music, costumes, dialect and cuisine. Dog-pulled wagons were a popular children's attraction in the 1970s.

Meeting Santa Claus at a costume party in kindergarten.

With my younger sister, Ashka, in a wintry Gliwice.

On holiday in the 1970s at our summer house in rural Bielsko-Biała, with my entire family: my grandmothers, Helunia and Genia; my grandfather, Gucio; my parents, Adam and Marta; my brother and sister; my mother's brother, Renik; his wife, Krystyna; and their daughter, Zofia. I never wondered why there were so few of us.

In front of St Mark's Basilica in Venice in August 1981, a holiday and a necessary ploy that set the stage for our escape from Poland a month later.

With my siblings, mother and grandmother at St Lucia, May 1982: our first holiday in a new country. Memorable for getting completely lost in the Maphelane Nature Reserve and seeing our first crocodile at the Crocodile Centre in St Lucia.

In my Pretoria High School for Girls formal uniform in Grade 9, 1986. I received my first academic badge in Grade 7, a year and a half after arriving in South Africa speaking only Polish.

With my sister and brother at Rhodes Memorial, Cape Town, January 1988. The family transferred to Cape Town in December 1987 ahead of my starting at the University of Cape Town with a bursary to study actuarial science.

The infamous national costume competition I was 'conned' into participating in at the Community Chest Carnival in 1989. It came with its own float parade through the centre of Cape Town.

I graduated from UCT in December 1991 with a Bachelor of Business Science (Actuarial Science) degree with distinction.

With Simon on our wedding day, 16 March 1997.

My grandparents, Gucio and Helunia Wierzycki (Getreu), Bielsko-Biała, Poland, 1999. They remained together until the end.

Skiing in Klosters, Switzerland, 2007. Some of our best family holidays have involved skiing.

An avid fan of cycling, I completed five Cape Town Cycle Tours. I finished another one with a broken elbow and blood streaming down my leg after a nasty fall.

Sygnia's over-the-top year-end staff parties were always an opportunity to dress up. From left: me, my brother Wojtek and his wife Trish Jorge, November 2016.

Sygnia Limited listed on the Johannesburg Stock Exchange on 14 October 2015, my birthday. Sygnia team from left: Louw Rabie, Willem van der Merwe, Niki Giles, Simon Peile, me, Iain Anderson, Andrew Steyn, Ashka Corelli, Wojtek Wierzycki, Dave Johnson, Trish Jorge and Riaan Brand.

Marching with the Sygnia team, my mother and thousands of South Africans across the country in April 2017, calling for President Jacob Zuma to step down after he fired finance minister Pravin Gordhan. Sygnia had special T-shirts and placards made for the occasion, which we turned into a team-building event.

Marching in support of a vote of no confidence in President Jacob Zuma, carrying balloons saying 'Vote Country Over Party', in August 2017. A sea of white and blue balloons floated above the gathered protesters in front of the Parliament buildings as we handed them out to everyone who asked.

As I am an avid lover of art, all our offices are modelled on art galleries. Johannesburg office, January 2018.

My parents, Marta and Adam Wierzycki, on Camps Bay Beach, March 2018. When they escaped from Poland, they left their own lives behind, to give us a better future.

With my sons Alex and Nicholas in front of St Mark's Basilica in August 2020. Whenever I'm in Venice, I always pose for a photo in the same spot I did in August 1981 before my family escaped from Poland. It puts in perspective just how short life is.

Meeting Lech Wałęsa, former leader of Solidarity, president of Poland and Nobel Peace Prize recipient, in Gdańsk, August 2021.

for women to be respected; they would offer suggestions, be there when required, guide their daughters to choose wisely, and support them in their struggles. I have seen too many men dismiss their daughters and put all their energy and ambitions into their sons. This is so easy to do, as teenage boys generally tend to bond with their fathers over common interests such as sport. Men may find it more difficult to bond over their daughters' love of fashion, for example. But every father should consciously look beyond the teenage years and ask himself whether he minds his daughter being treated in the workplace the way he possibly treats his female colleagues or sees them being treated by others. If the answer is no, then he is compelled to step in and advise. I wish someone had intervened on my behalf at Coronation. I was very young to be put through all that. I learnt many lessons, but the experience left just as many scars.

Having acknowledged and accepted that women must work harder than men, I did not run away from it and I did not complain. I am a pragmatist. There is no point wasting energy on something that cannot be easily changed. So I worked harder than most men I know. And with that work came an accumulation of skills and knowledge that would one day allow me to build my own business. Having said that, you do need to demand the recognition due to you. One reason men achieve more despite working less is that, whenever they achieve something, no matter how insignificant, they tell everyone about it. Women just put their heads down and get on with it, hoping that the recognition will follow. Well, it doesn't. Standing up for yourself might result in a breakdown in your relationship with your employer, but if it does, you need to ask yourself whether this is the kind of company or person you want to work for. If they do not acknowledge your contribution now, what makes you think this will change? Rather reconsider your options.

There is no escaping the fact that women are different from men. As I've said before, in my experience women are more emotional, they loathe conflict, and they prefer collaboration to being 'lone wolves' hunting only for themselves. Yet they can multitask, they work harder than men to prove themselves, and they are more loyal, provided you create a flexible and supportive work environment. I shed many a tear at Coronation. I am not ashamed of that. Over time, however, as a woman I had to develop a thick skin.

As a concrete, and humorous, illustration of the differences between men and women's ways of working, I have to look no further than a team-building event I attended in the African Harvest days. We were taken to a rural part of South Africa and given the task of shepherding sheep through an obstacle course. We split into two teams, women versus men. Without any prior experience, the women managed to guide the sheep through the obstacle course within twenty minutes. Then we sat back and watched with bemusement as the men chased their sheep through the field. Needless to say, none made it through the obstacle course. The odds were always stacked against the men, though. The keyword to success in this instance is exactly what distinguishes women from men in the workplace: collaboration. As women, we designed a plan of action before throwing ourselves into the execution. We did not try to compete with one another. Forming a semicircle and working together, we calmly guided our sheep where they needed to go. For the men, it was every man for himself. They adopted the 'lone wolf' strategy, each man chasing his own sheep. Sheep are skittish. They scatter when chased. It was not surprising that none of them completed the course.

While men tend to be mystified by our strengths in certain areas, they have learnt how to exploit our weaknesses. When it comes to dealing with a woman's demands, men will get personal, like my boss at Coronation did during my biannual performance reviews. They will use words such as 'oversensitive', 'erratic', 'irrational', 'neurotic' and 'emotional'. What they really mean is that they do not, and don't want to, see you as an equal. Of course, when criticised, women tend to apologise and promise to do better. We're immediately put on the back foot. This tactic will not work with men, because a man will simply bang the table and say, 'Who cares what others think? Let's talk about that salary increase.' It took me many years to figure this one out. I have never personally experienced women in the workplace being oversensitive, erratic, irrational, neurotic or emotional. I have, however, seen men display these characteristics, and worse, when it comes to money.

Women are also more vulnerable to intimidation and exploitation. This is why it's so important for us, as women, to recognise our weaknesses and address them. We must also learn to set our own goals and boundaries and stick to them. It is crucial for every woman to realise that her limits are her own to determine. Despite my experiences, I am still learning to set my own boundaries. A very successful male friend has repeatedly told me to live by the maxim 'If it's not an obvious yes, just say no.' I recently asked another male friend who is excellent at setting boundaries to teach me how he sets his personal boundaries. He repeated the same mantra: just say no to requests without feeling the need to explain. I tend to say yes to everything, however unreasonable the demand. If I do say no, I intuitively feel guilty, apologise and provide lengthy explanations. Invariably, I end up with too many things on my plate. I think that is true of most women.

As I climbed higher up the corporate ladder, I became a bigger target – mostly of jealousy and other people's insecurities. I had to learn to accept that I would be criticised, and then how to handle it. Today, if the criticism relates to real work issues, I try to consider it and learn from it rather than become defensive. If it is personal, no matter the source, I ignore it immediately. It took me a long time to get to this point, and I wish I had known enough to do just that at Coronation.

Over time, I have also become more circumspect in what I share with others. Recently, someone described me to a colleague as 'an antidepressant-addicted alcoholic' after I told him that I take epilepsy medication that is often prescribed as an antidepressant and joked about needing a glass of wine a day due to the Covid-19 pandemic. He did so in anger over some issue I would not give in on, and it was an extreme case of a storm in a teacup, but this episode reminded me not to share too many personal things with colleagues, even in jest, that can be distorted and turned against me in another forum.

Women, especially those in senior positions, are also at a disadvantage in terms of support. Male executives drink together, play golf, talk about sport. Because there are typically a limited number of spaces in senior management for women, aspirant female executives will often undermine and criticise one another. They seldom lend more junior women a help-ing hand, let alone mentorship. This is incredibly destructive to women's progress in the workplace. Once you have reached a certain position, you need to get over your insecurities and recognise that the only way you will progress higher – apart from courting the approval of the men above you, and the support of the men below you, which you will seldom get – is if you have the support of the women below you, cheering you on. This requires women to create their own networks early on. At the start it must be made clear to all participants that these support networks will be used to facilitate female progression within the organisation as women in senior positions begin pulling women up behind them, as men have done for decades. Over time it should become self-evident. I recognised early on that I would never be accepted into the 'alpha-male' ranks; I would have to form my own pack. Incidentally, that pack today consists of like-minded women, as well as men.

While support networks take time to build and nurture, there are some practical areas in which women can make changes that will return more immediate dividends. I was advising a woman in a senior fund management position when it occurred to me that one of the problems with her approach was the length of her emails. Her emails spanned pages. I remember doing the same at Coronation, fully expecting that someone would read them, particularly if they were about unfair treatment. Guess what? No one did. As I skimmed her emails, reading only the opening and closing paragraphs, it struck me that men don't write prose. They write in shorthand and bullet points, without emotion. They tend to come across as brusque, but they get their point across much more efficiently and effectively. Ladies, it's time to shorten those emails. If you can't summar-ise what you want to say in five bullet points, rewrite it until you can.

It's also important to try to stand out from the crowd. I do not wear black clothes to work, and I never try to emulate the male uniform of suit and tie. I always wear colourful clothing. Monotone to preserve professionalism, but colourful, be it bright red, canary yellow or electric blue. No crazy patterns, short skirts or low necklines. Optics matter. In a room full of similarly dressed people, I always stand out from the crowd. In my experience, dressing professionally, albeit with flair, being proficient, having a constructive approach to problem-solving and keeping an emotional distance from colleagues are all great tools. Gossiping, shifting blame, avoiding responsibility and forming cliques are not. And never assume that the person in charge is an idiot. They may not know the details, but they can quickly assess who does what and reward accordingly. No one will pay you or promote you for using company time to browse social media.

As the world has become more chaotic and fraught with risk, more women have risen to the top. In the political arena, across the globe, there have been Theresa May, Angela Merkel, Christine Lagarde, Ursula von der Leyen, Ellen Johnson Sirleaf, Tomomi Inada, Joyce Banda, Sahle-Work Zewde and Jacinta Ardern, to name a few. In the corporate world there have been Marissa Mayer, parachuted in to save a failing Yahoo, and Sheryl Sandberg, the chief operating officer of Meta (Facebook). These women were brought in when the going got tough. I think one of the reasons the world turns to powerful women is that they have always had it tough and have risen to the top nonetheless. They inspire confidence, command respect and can be trusted to get the job done.

During the 2016 US presidential election, as Donald Trump stumbled from one gaffe to another, Hillary Clinton explained patiently how she sweats the details of policy and gets the job done. As Michael Gove and Boris Johnson backstabbed each other in the 2016 Tory leadership race, the Conservative Party turned to Theresa May as the only person capable of getting them through the Brexit mess. It doesn't matter the outcome for both women. The fact that they were there, on the global stage, was a giant step forward.

There have been some changes in the financial services industry since I joined it almost twenty-five years ago. Unfortunately, a lot has stayed the same. There are still very few women in senior positions, albeit many more than when I was young. I think this is a function of both personal choice and low levels of acceptance in the workplace. A friend of mine was recently sidelined by a large investment management company by being given a lofty title with an empty job description heading nowhere. At the end of the day, she decided to accept her 'lot in life', notwithstanding being one of the most talented and intelligent people I know. My instinct would have been to fight, but I was advised by someone I respect not to project my own ambitions onto other women. That gave me food for thought.

Despite the challenges and obstacles, I would not give up on the financial services sector. It's a tough environment, but it's also very satisfying. People are entrusting you with their life savings. It is a huge responsibility and a service to humanity. Done right, it enables people to enjoy a stress-free life, buy property and retire in comfort. While some women complain that they are surrounded by greed and that their work life has no true meaning, I don't agree. The role the financial services industry fulfils is essential to the economy. This was acknowledged during the pandemic, when the sector was classified as an essential service as it is entrusted with paying benefits, including pensions, managing savings and protecting the economy from collapse.

The financial services industry is not a job creator in the classical sense. It will never employ masses of people, particularly in emerging markets where skills and education are limited to the most privileged. But it is the glue that holds the economy together. And we can make a significant difference by focusing on customers' interests rather than profits, by educating people about the importance of saving and investing, by working collaboratively, and by using our skills beyond the constraints of the job. In my own life, I present and lecture to young people, I write articles on finance and other topics of interest in simple language, and I support deserving students through bursaries. I have recently started giving ad hoc lectures on ethical leadership at Columbia University's Business School in New York. It amazes me that the messages I convey have global relevance.

I have steered away from one-on-one mentorship as I want to spread my skills and limited time more widely than to a single individual. Interestingly, I've been approached for mentorship by more men than women. My advice to people who need support is to use life coaches. They can help you to identify your weaknesses, to grow, to learn how to respond in work situations and to interpret what is happening around you. Preferably find a life coach yourself and don't rely on one provided by your organisation. One large financial services company based in South Africa made a life coach available to its executive staff and then demanded full access to the information they disclosed to the coach. Life coaches are not therapists; they are not there to support you. They are there to toughen you up and enable you to make your own decisions. I think this is why I have always liked the idea of a life coach with a military background.

I often wonder whether I have fully embraced all the lessons I've learnt. I still get upset when someone attacks me personally, but I have taught myself not to cry. Being an empathetic person, I am vulnerable to manipulation. Less so today, but there are some clever manipulators and exploiters out there who are expert at hiding that side of their personality until it's too late. I continue to work harder than most. I struggle to say no. I don't think I've shattered any glass ceilings, but I have broken the mould by being a female entrepreneur in the financial services industry. If that inspires other women, then that is achievement enough.

13

The Birth of Sygnia

THE CONCLUSION OF THE AFRICAN HARVEST transaction at the end of September 2006 meant that I was financially secure for the first time in my life. This would have been a good time to pause, take a breath and plan what to do next. Perhaps it was the adrenaline rush of the deal, or the panic I feel whenever I'm faced with a potential void, but I had already set something in motion by the time I boarded a plane to London to celebrate with Mzi. When I met him for dinner, I proudly showed him my present to myself – a platinum Rolex watch that I still wear today. He inspected it carefully, then shook his head and said, 'Magda, you really don't know how to be rich.'

The problem was that I wasn't rich. All the money I had made from the African Harvest deal was invested in a new, yet-to-be-named venture. I didn't have a plan or a real business strategy, but I did have a group of incredible people around me, with a diversity of skills and talents unmatched in the industry.

It all came about when, midway through the African Harvest transaction, my intrepid CFO came to me to ask what we were all going to do next. Of course, it was a question I had been asking for a while, but in relation to my own future. I obviously wanted to know who 'we' were. 'We' turned out to be a long list of African Harvest staff members who refused to be 'sold' and were ready to pursue a new venture. While I encourage people to dream, I also think risk-taking is the domain of those touched by madness, particularly if the risk affects your livelihood. Looking at the list of people, I knew that a lot of them, despite their enthusiasm, could not afford to take the kind of risks a new venture posed. I believe in taking calculated risks, and betting your future on someone else's potential success does not fit this strategy. In the end, whether motivated by adrenaline or panic, I eventually agreed to the new, unspecified venture, but with a more modest list of people with a particular range of skills.

As a believer that perception matters as much as reality, at least in the short term, I went off in search of cheap but impressive office space. I found a gem at Cape Town's V&A Waterfront. The original harbour master's house needed a lot of work, and was a historical monument, but it had panoramic views of the Waterfront all the way to the Atlantic Ocean and a giant cricket lawn in front. As a self-anointed interior decorator, I never worry about the interior. Walls can be repainted or moved, new carpets can be laid and new lighting installed. It is the foundation, structure and setting that matter.

While I was embroiled in negotiating the African Harvest sale, my most trusted staff were chasing up builders, repainting offices and preparing our new premises. At least this time, unlike with IQvest, I had some capital to throw behind the endeavour.

We also needed a name for the business, which came after we developed the tagline and logo. Because I praise teamwork above all else in business, and firmly believe you can move mountains as a team, I came up with the tagline 'a sum of all things', premised on the idea that the team is always stronger than the individual. Once we had a tagline, the natural next step was to design a logo. The word 'sum' led us to the sigma sign (Σ). But you cannot trademark the sigma sign. I hired a great design firm of ex-South Africans based in London and asked them to convert the symbol into something special that reflected Africa. They tilted the sigma and embedded the shape of the African continent in it to create a really iconic design. Once we had the logo, we needed a name. The same team came up with over a hundred different made-up names, and Sygnia stood out. Many companies don't spend enough time or effort on design, branding and naming. But having learnt early on that humans are visual creatures, I spend an inordinate amount of time on design. In my opinion, it matters.

I often say that to be successful you need to love what you do. To love what you do, you need to ensure that your career merges 'real work' with things you are passionate about and would normally define as 'hobbies'. I love graphic design and art, and so have become very involved in marketing. I design my own slide presentations, including layouts. I let my imagination roam through content while my fingers produce beautiful pictures. I also love interior design and have been involved in decorating each Sygnia office, choosing everything from light fittings, desk designs and bar coasters to the shape and colour of office chairs.

We moved into our new offices on 1 November 2006, a month after closing the African Harvest deal. When I sat down with my freshly minted team, I may not have had a business plan, but I had something more powerful. I had complete freedom. For the first time in my career, I had an opportunity to create a company from scratch, infused with my own values and beliefs, with people I liked and respected, and who, in turn, liked and respected me.

I had a logo, a name, beautiful premises and a team of truly enthusiastic and talented people raring to go: my assistant Ronel and quantitative analyst Willem, who had both followed me from Coronation; my husband, Simon, in the role of head of investments; genius coder Joseph from IQvest with our fairly rudimentary administration system software; and my chief financial officer, Niki, head of administration Aisha Couturier and 'IT guy' Rory Gillan from African Harvest. (A couple of people from Coronation joined soon after.) What I did not have, as already mentioned, was a business. I had to invent one from scratch.

I believe that to succeed as an entrepreneur you need to innovate and not imitate. Many of the most successful businesses in history have been premised on this belief. Companies such as Facebook, Amazon, Zoom, and, closer to home, Discovery and Liberty Life were all founded on a novel approach to the same market others were chasing.

If you imitate others, you are setting yourself up for failure. There is always someone ahead of you, with more capital, a longer track record and more resources. Playing catch-up is difficult. Innovation is easier, provided you're a dreamer. Whenever I start a business or come up with an idea, I haul out the whiteboard and ask: 'If there were no restrictions whatsoever, what would the best-of-breed business, service or product look like?' Normally there are some basic criteria, such as it must meet a real need, be affordable, and be fair to clients and the business. But beyond that, I let the experts in the field guide the design and the discussion. To innovate you need courage. You know that you will make mistakes and go down a few blind alleys. The problem lies not in making mistakes, but in being able to acknowledge that you have done so and change track in time. I am the first one to say, 'I made a mistake. This is on me.' The idea is to instil in other people the courage to do the same and know that there will be no consequences if you admit to an error. There will be if you try to hide it. I have made many mistakes. I rush to judgement, I make off-the-cuff decisions, I throw money at problems. I know my weaknesses and I'll only work with people who are not afraid to stand up to me. While to outsiders it may look like I dominate, I seldom do. The team dynamic is foreign to people who believe that standing up to someone involves raising your voice, banging the table and becoming aggressive, as I have witnessed so many times over the years. A friend with an investment banking background once told me that every day he went to the office to fight a battle. I have never gone to the office to fight. I go to the office to enjoy myself; it is my 'home away from home'. During the Covid-19 pandemic, while we let most of our staff work from home, I went to the office almost every day. It kept me sane.

Given that Sygnia was a new venture, supported by nothing other than some capital from Simon and me, we needed to be creative in terms of what products and services we offered. We also had to be flexible. Our business model would evolve over time. We were about to take on the mighty financial services industry with no assets beyond our reputations, little real capital behind us, no performance track record and no clients bar a handful from IQvest whose assets we managed on an index tracking basis. On that first day, we sat around the table and brainstormed over the noise of the seagulls on the lawn outside our boardroom. The topic under discussion was how to disrupt the financial services industry. The answer was amazingly simple. Make financial services simple and understandable. Eliminate all the jargon. Ensure that everything shown to a client is easy to interpret. And, most importantly, lower the cost of saving and investing. Lower it a lot. Cut the fat and leave the skeleton. And be realistic about who you can hope to displace.

Often, companies that survive and thrive over time are those that do not focus on maximising profits, but instead on a commitment to a greater cause. In our case that greater cause became creating value for our clients, ahead of making profits. This cause has guided Sygnia since its founding. It serves as our moral compass and conscience, and it enables us to think strategically and make decisions for the long term, unconcerned with short-term incentives.

We lived what we preached. Simon and I did not draw a salary from Sygnia for several years, living off our savings and our mortgage bond. This enabled us to scale up the business. In the sixteen years I ran Sygnia as its chief executive, I received only one bonus, in the final year before stepping down. Until that point, I took a minimal salary by market standards and reinvested in the company.

Showing commitment to our cause, we built Sygnia on the promise of very low fees in respect of all the products we offered. I have seen first-hand the consequences of high management fees. My uncle, also a Polish refugee who followed us to South Africa with his family, is a very disciplined man. He started saving immediately on arrival in the country through a savings product 'sold' to him by a financial advisor employed by a large insurance company. After twenty-five years of saving, he expected to retire in some comfort. But when he saw the final amount printed on his retirement benefit statement, the associated stress caused him to have a heart attack a few months later. Twenty-five years of rigorous saving had translated into little more than two years' worth of his annual salary just before retirement. Most of his savings had been eroded by poor returns and high fees. That experience was at the back of my mind when we developed the strategy for Sygnia. Every business needs to make a profit. There is nothing wrong with that. The trick is to design a business model where profit does not come at the expense of people who trust you. The fees for whatever you are selling or offering should be fair. That is all. Unfortunately, the financial services industry, and investment banking in particular, is full of people driven by greed. A lot of them were exposed in the wake of the global financial crisis and many firms are still reeling from the consequences. I could have made a lot more money if I had been greedier, if I had priced our products at higher levels, or if I had been willing to pay bribes to secure business.

I have been exposed to several different investment approaches over the years, from active investment management (at Coronation and African Harvest) to passive investing and hedge funds (at IQvest and Sygnia) to venture capital investing (at Braavos Investment Advisers in the UK, where I am currently a general partner). For the average investor who has little interest in investment markets, I firmly believe that passive investing is the way to go. For those more interested in finance, a mixture of passive investing and venture capital and private markets investing offers the best returns. I will undoubtedly be criticised for my stance as I am involved in both, but my answer to the critics is that I would never launch a product unless I believed in it and invested my own money in the same manner. I have the freedom to offer anything I want to investors. I choose to offer what I believe will serve them best.

The field of investing is complicated and typically requires professional financial advice. The recent emergence of share trading platforms such as Robinhood is terrifying. Given that most day traders are amateurs with no idea what they are doing, their activities can only be described as glorified gambling. A real investor makes educated decisions about how best to mix different assets in your savings account, whether to switch asset classes over time, what investment managers to choose, whether to broaden your investment basket to include other, more complex strategies, and so on. If you choose not to seek professional advice, you need to educate yourself. Neither of my sons wants to take over running Sygnia, or even pursue a career in finance. However, they are both likely to inherit money, so I have struck a deal with them. They have committed to 'giving' me a year of their life in their twenties to study for an MBA. Being financially literate is an essential life skill.

Sygnia gave me the platform to call myself an entrepreneur. Being an entrepreneur is hard work, particularly in a country such as South Africa, where there are few investors willing to take the financial risk of supporting a start-up. Every day my inbox is flooded with business proposals from people who have designed or developed a new product or service, or have a novel idea, but who need financial support. I wish I had the time and skills to evaluate each one. Unfortunately, I am just one person with a full-time job, or a few jobs now that I have moved on from being CEO of Sygnia.

I am acutely aware that the world outside South Africa is awash with money to support new businesses. A lot of that money is chasing ideas and concepts, rather than tangible returns on investment. It's a very different environment to the one I encountered when launching IQvest and Sygnia. But however plentiful, all this money has only created a handful of real entrepreneurs. Most start-ups, repeatedly funded by venture capital firms in exchange for a shareholding in the business, are rapidly taken over by professional management teams. The ownership stakes of the 'founders' who had the original idea are quickly and significantly diluted. It's the price you pay for being funded by other people's money. But that is not true entrepreneurship. True entrepreneurs do not easily give up stakes in their own companies. They would rather make sacrifices and take real financial risks than repeatedly replenishing the coffers with other people's money. That is what gives them the motivation to succeed.

In South Africa, what often passes for entrepreneurship is far from it. An article from the *Financial Mail* dated 20 March 2007, six months after Sygnia was launched, demonstrates this. Titled 'Stellenbosch has thrived as home for SA's Afrikaner business elite', the article illustrates how all these powerful (white) businessmen are linked to one another and support each other with capital and connections. They aren't true entrepreneurs in that they've never had to take risks or fight for their survival.

The most important lessons on entrepreneurship that I have learnt through experience are the same lessons my father tried to impart to me when I was a teenager. The key one is not to depend on anyone but yourself. This has served me well in a world where, as I've mentioned, women have no networks to provide support and no mentorship of the type described in the *Financial Mail* article. Men leverage endless rounds of golf, memberships at exclusive men's clubs and school connections to get ahead in the business world. Women have nothing similar. As much as this did not bother me at the time, I believe that women need to create their own networks. And I don't mean book clubs and coffee dates, but semi-social events dedicated exclusively to the exchange of ideas and experiences in a work environment.

Having said that, being independent meant that I did not owe any-one my allegiance. I could say what I wanted when I wanted. I was able to speak up against state capture when others stayed silent. I could make decisions even if they were costly to Sygnia, drew criticism and upset the status quo.

In the absence of real capital, where does one start? I started with the money in my mortgage bond. That is what enabled me to set up IQvest and acquire shares in African Harvest, which then allowed me to fund Sygnia's birth. As I've said, I am a proponent of taking calculated risks, and I have always viewed betting on myself as a risk worth taking. Conse-quently, I backed myself and my ideas. If I failed, I would fail on my own dime.

Our decision early on in our careers to take out a mortgage bond on a house we truly could not afford, and then repay it as quickly as possible, turned out to be critical to our success. While property often does not provide the same returns that investment markets can deliver, it offers several secondary benefits, including a stable, enjoyable lifestyle, and a method of forced saving. When not investing in a business, we focused on our bond repayments. When an opportunity arose to acquire more shares in African Harvest, we used our access bond facility to do so. This was a risk, but a calculated one. I would never recommend accessing bond financing to take risks unless you are in full control of the delivery. Once we sold African Harvest, our investment multiplied manyfold, providing start-up capital for Sygnia. Sygnia would not exist without the properties we invested in and the mortgages we had access to.

Most entrepreneurs know that there are no shortcuts to success and that to succeed you need to disrupt the status quo. From the beginning, we positioned Sygnia as a 'market disruptor' in the South African financial services industry. But what does that mean in practice? The theory of 'disruptive innovation' was first formulated by Harvard Business School professor Clayton Christensen in the 1990s. The theory is premised on the idea that true innovation transforms an existing market by introducing simplicity, convenience, accessibility and affordability where complexity and high costs are the status quo.

It is not that traditional companies do not innovate. The problem is that to compete with others they tend to innovate in a more complex manner than necessarily meets their customers' needs. They offer products and services that are too sophisticated, too expensive and too complicated. To maintain profits, they then end up concentrating their efforts on customers who are willing and able to pay the highest prices. This opens the door for disruptive innovators who offer the same products in a simplified form and at a lower cost, initially to the market ignored by large companies and eventually to everyone.

'The innovation transforms something that used to be so costly, only the very rich had access to it,' Christensen told *Harvard Magazine* in 2014. 'These innovations make it so affordable and simple that normal people can do what only the rich and very skilled could do before.'

Uber, Airbnb and Amazon are the most often quoted examples of disruption. All three essentially displaced an existing market by providing a service that was more efficient and cost-effective. The rest is history.

Disruption and innovation are not the same thing. All disruptors are innovators, but not all innovators are disruptors. Disruption is also not competition. Traditional competitors fight one another, offering the same product to the same target market. Disruptors do not compete against other suppliers. They compete against 'non-consumption' by creating new consumers and new demand. The Covid-19 pandemic created a perfect environment for disruption. Software such as Zoom and Microsoft Teams replaced the need for face-to-face meetings and travel. Given the convenience and low cost of this form of engagement, combined with greater time efficiency, it is unlikely that business will revert completely to its old ways.

Applying the philosophy of disruptive innovation to Sygnia, we targeted a number of industries with the 'financial services' label. On the multi-management front, where companies offer investment products premised on appointing multiple investment managers and 'wrapping' them in one convenient product, we offered a new service. We gave retirement funds the option of designing their own customised investment strategies, rather than buying off-the-shelf products. This brought a lot of transparency to a traditionally opaque industry.

On the investment management front, we launched index tracking funds at less than half the cost of an actively managed alternative. We initially blended index tracking funds with third-party active investment managers to attract clients with lower fees than our competitors. Eventually the time came to offer products based solely on index tracking strategies, which enabled us to offer investment products at an even lower fee than before.

On the savings front, we started offering savings wrappers, such as retirement annuities and living annuities, for free if the assets were invested with Sygnia, reducing the cost of saving to a quarter of that of a traditional proposition if the investor chose an index tracking fund. In terms of retirement, we introduced an innovative umbrella fund. Umbrella funds are used by companies that no longer want the inconvenience of running a standalone retirement fund for their employees and do not mind buying an off-the-shelf fund offering from a financial services company. Ours was truly unique in that it did not layer fees by charging separate administration, consulting and investment fees. Members paid one fee only, the investment management fee, which translated into an almost seventy per cent discount on what established umbrella funds were charging.

On the advisory front, we launched the first robo-advisor in the country to provide simple and clear investment advice for free via our website on a no-obligation basis. Financial advisors are necessary if your affairs are complicated or if you have a lot of money. But if your affairs are simple, or if you are young, using an automated service to design your investment strategy or at least educate you about savings is an astute and cost-free move.

I cannot overstate the impact of management fees and charges on your savings and investments over time. My favourite quote comes from a well-researched National Treasury discussion paper published in 2013 titled 'Charges in South African retirement funds'. It states that 'a regular saver who reduces the charges on his retirement account from 2.5 per cent of assets each year to 0.5 per cent of assets annually would receive a benefit 60 per cent greater at retirement after 40 years, all else being equal'. I use this quote in almost every seminar I give. Imagine retiring with R1.6 million instead of R1 million. That is a substantial difference. As a rule of thumb, if a management fee exceeds one per cent, avoid the product, however enticing it looks. There is a perception that private equity and venture capital managers charge higher fees. It is just a perception. The management fees are calculated in a very different manner to that of traditional listed investments, and are in fact fairly modest unless the managers deliver extraordinary returns.

It is astounding how easy it has been to become a market disruptor. The financial services industry in South Africa has remained largely unaffected by change despite the global financial crisis. The same players, the same products, the same high and often hidden fees, all competing for the same customers. This has left the field wide open for someone to come along and upset the status quo by lowering the cost, improving the product proposition, bringing more transparency to the industry and simplifying access. The challenge to the industry is to respond. But can it? All established financial services companies have existing revenue streams, shareholder expectations and staff bonuses to pay. The only way to respond would be to cut all these by at least half. I'm not holding my breath.

Being a market disruptor has its downsides, though. Unless you realise that whatever is innovative today is likely to become a commodity over time and focus on evolving and coming up with new ideas, you are likely to be imitated or, worse, disrupted yourself.

14

Building a Brand

A S I HAVE ALREADY SAID, starting a new business requires hard work. But many people work really hard without ever reaping any benefits. Beyond stamina, you also need a healthy dose of good luck. Our good luck was a result of our investment in developing new administration software. At inception, we decided we would need a system that would meet the specific needs of an investment management company that managed money directly as well as by appointing outside investment managers. To this end, Joseph developed a software system that quite incidentally fitted into an administrative niche not met by any other software or administration service provider in the market. Knowledge of our newly developed system spread sufficiently widely that several large companies, including a US-based financial services group, approached us with a view to licensing the system.

We did our homework and quickly learnt that licensing software is a fool's game, particularly when dealing with complex administration. Whatever mistakes licensees make are invariably blamed on the system, which then requires a team of support staff to resolve. And so we decided against licensing and turned down several lucrative contracts. It was not an easy decision for a small company that made no revenue, but that is one of the strengths of working as a team. We all debated the merits of the licensing model, we all went some way towards entering negotiations, and we all agreed to walk away when faced with the inevitable 'support and maintenance' legal agreements.

A couple of these companies, however, came back and asked if we would take them on as administration-only clients. We hadn't really thought of providing administration-only services, but once we looked at the size of the assets involved, we found no reason why we could not pivot the business. The profit margins were small, as our first two clients were giant institutions, and we literally worked day and night to onboard them onto the system. But the benefit of being willing to broaden the scope of our offering beyond investment management services meant that we suddenly had substantial clients who could act as references for future business. Another valuable lesson in those early days was that you cannot underestimate the impact of referrals. Individuals and institutions look at who else has used or appointed your company. Today, most company websites carry client reviews, but back then Sygnia was one of the first to recognise their value.

Administration aside, we focused on how best to structure financial products for institutional investors and retirement funds that met our criteria of transparency, simplicity and affordability, as well as a market need. We knew we wanted to disrupt and thus had to design something that would stand out from the crowd. At the same time, however, the 'standing out' could not be so extreme that we would not attract any clients. Disruption doesn't happen overnight. It is a slow process of changing mindsets and prodding decision-makers towards your desired outcome. Given my experiences with active investment management, I knew that I never again wanted to work with difficult, money-oriented people.

There was one incident in the early days of Sygnia that pulled me right back into that unpleasant world. It was also my first brush with the legal system. When I took over African Harvest, I had to replace a senior manager. I hired someone I knew in the industry, but I should have done better research. It soon became apparent that he did very little work, disappearing from the office for hours at a time almost every day. When I confronted him, he asked me how much I was prepared to pay him to go quietly. He had apparently done this before with other employers. He said he would drown me in paperwork until I complied. I immediately hired lawyers and he was dismissed after a lengthy disciplinary process. During that period, I was told that he liked to indulge in drugs, and I naively repeated this to a few people. Almost three years later, after I had made some money from the sale of African Harvest, he opportunistically sued me for defamation. He claimed that, while he did use marijuana, I had implied that he used cocaine. Irrespective of whether his claim had any merit, I soon learnt that the legal fees of taking a matter to court often far outweigh any potential benefit. I got as far as the steps of the High Court on the morning of the proceedings before my lawyers persuaded me to settle.

As I lost faith in active investment management, my passion for index tracking as a way of managing money grew. It is diversified, it is cheap, it can last a lifetime as a strategy, and it is highly effective in delivering good performance. Unfortunately, back in 2006, South African investors were not ready for 100 per cent index tracking products. Even today, almost twenty years later, many still resist.

I put South Africa's reluctance to adopt index tracking, which has upended the investment management industry in the US, down to years of marketing and advertising by active investment managers. Hundreds of millions of rands have been spent over the years on self-promotion. From television advertisements to billboards at airports, everyone claims to be an exceptionally skilled top performer with a long-term focus. Think about that. If everyone is a top performer, who did they beat? No one can stay on top forever. It is enough to look at the inconsistency of perform-ance generated by active investment managers over time to realise that exceptional skills are rare. And 'long-term' must be inserted into every advert to brush over those short-term cycles of bad performance that every investment manager regularly experiences.

You cannot underestimate the power of advertising. When I asked my then seventy-year-old mother, a medical doctor with no financial experi-ence, which investment manager in South Africa she would invest her money with, she immediately answered, 'Allan Gray.' Allan Gray is one of South Africa's largest investment management companies and the first to recognise the exponential power of advertising. They have spent a lot of money perfecting their marketing over the years. Others followed much later, just to discover that the ticket to the game had got more expensive. To make a difference, they had to spend more than Allan Gray. Being the first and an innovator in the field gave Allan Gray an advantage in that the average person could immediately associate their brand with investment management, just like Ford became synonymous with cars and Netflix with online streaming.

For a small business with a negligible advertising budget, breaking through the subliminal bias can seem almost impossible. Once again, we needed to innovate, rather than imitate.

The first step was to design products that were an acceptable compromise for investors but innovative enough to attract attention. Each product featured a mix of index tracking strategies and funds managed by well-known investment management houses. Using recognised investment managers instantly gave Sygnia's products credibility. Essentially, we leveraged the well-established brands of our competitors to boost confidence in Sygnia. This turned out to be the right strategy to attract institutional investors. They liked the fact that we lowered the costs of their investments and took comfort that a big part of their money would still be managed by brands they knew and trusted.

There is nothing wrong with leveraging. The best advert I remember from my youth was one in which BMW took on Mercedes-Benz. Mercedes had filmed an advert showing how well their vehicle survived falling down a cliff after badly navigating a particularly sharp bend on Chapman's Peak Drive. BMW replicated the scene, but instead of going off the cliff, the BMW smoothly negotiated the bend. The tagline, 'BMW beats the bends', earned them an immediate fine from the Competition Commission as competitive advertising is not permitted in South Africa, but it was worth every cent. The publicity they received was massive.

Apparently, some of Sygnia's competitors have complained to the regulators about the fact that I frequently compare the performance of active investment managers to that of index tracking funds on social media platforms. These complaints have gone nowhere, unfortunately, as I'm sure that, like BMW, Sygnia would receive an incredible boost from the inevitable publicity that would follow.

When designing a product or service, you cannot fall in love with your ideas. Ideas that may seem obvious to you might not meet a particular need in the market. There is also a risk that they are not as inventive as you thought. Be pragmatic in terms of your business model and product or service offering. If your idea does not gain traction, you need to be able to pivot to something that does. It took us five years from inception to muster the courage to launch a 100 per cent index tracking product range. One of our competitors entered with an exclusive index tracking offering too soon and became almost evangelical in their marketing approach. They tried to bully the market into their way of thinking, rather than taking the time to educate investors, and failed miserably as a result. Too many businesses fail, or fail to thrive, by not taking the realities of their target market into account.

The next step was to find alternative methods of becoming visible. Without a multimillion-rand budget, spending a cent on traditional advertising is a cent too much. It is impossible to outspend competitors to break through the noise. I have always believed that advertising and public relations are two sides of the same coin. Both get you exposure, but you pay for the first, whereas the second is free if done smartly and correctly. Getting newspapers and other distributors of news with access to eyeballs to feature your products and services without payment is difficult, but not impossible. It just requires an active strategy.

I can write, and I have strong opinions. If you can combine the two into articulate, easily understood articles, most newspapers and magazines are more than happy to publish them, either as opinion pieces or by writing their own articles using your content. Before Sygnia, I regularly wrote articles for business publications. As my confidence grew, my articles became less technical and more opinion oriented, and I realised that to promote Sygnia's brand was as easy as establishing myself in the minds of ordinary people as the 'CEO of Sygnia'. In this way, I created interest in Sygnia as a brand. Over time, more of my articles were picked up and distributed. These were the days before social media, when getting your message across was easier because people were still prepared to read

400 words. The emergence of platforms like Twitter and Instagram has made it more difficult today to have the same impact when your profile is reliant solely on public relations, as Sygnia's was in the early days. Perversely, the pandemic has given many businesses an opportunity to innovate. In terms of marketing, we realised that people stuck at home during lockdowns would have more time on their hands. We therefore started offering regular Zoom webinars for investors that we advertised on social media. These proved to be extremely popular. A few other companies adopted this approach, but, as it is extremely work intensive, many soon abandoned their efforts. We persisted.

I made one strategic error. I started the public relations campaign too late in Sygnia's evolution. Running African Harvest, as the only female CEO of an investment management company in South Africa, I received a fair amount of media coverage. Nothing like today, but enough to be tired of the anonymous online comments that appeared beneath my articles. I have since developed a motto: don't read the noise. Anonymous commentary is not worth a second of your time. The attacks in the early days were as brutal and sexist as they are today, so when we launched Sygnia, I decided to give media exposure a break. I told the team that we would not shout from the rooftops until we had something to shout about. For me, that moment came when we reached R100 billion in assets under management and administration. I wrote a press release about Sygnia and our size and sent it to all the newspapers. I expected an avalanche of phone calls. Instead, there was deafening silence. It turned out that most publications had not taken the press release seriously because no one could believe that a medium-sized financial services company had flown under everyone's radar. Eventually, one lone journalist got in touch to find out what we were all about. One interview led to another as more people woke up and asked, 'Who the hell is Sygnia? How can a company we have never heard of be managing R100 billion?' If I was going for the shock effect, I got it.

After the initial disbelief wore off, we were taken a lot more seriously and my self-penned articles on financial issues began to gain traction. With that traction came more brand recognition. We became a real 'player' in the investment management industry as far as institutional investors were concerned.

As our client base grew, so did our staff complement. We had worked hard to develop a strong organisational culture that we nurtured. To this end, we carefully screened new hires to ensure that they suited the culture of the company. Some people naturally fitted in, while others hated it. When it comes to hiring and firing, I am guided by a few basic principles. Anyone who tries too hard to ingratiate themselves with me raises an immediate red flag. If those people injected the same amount of effort into their work as they do into trying to impress me, they would be a lot more successful, at least in any company I manage. I look for the over-looked, the hard-working and the underdog, and try to give them the opportunities and recognition they would not otherwise get by virtue of not having flashy, demanding personalities. I believe in teamwork. I always say to my teams that if we want to fight, we fight our competitors. There are plenty of them out there. We do not fight internally. We work with one another, not against one another. I seldom use 'I', unless making a very strong point. I have trained myself to use 'we'.

You need to like and respect the people you work with. Lack of respect for colleagues is another red flag. As are people concerned with status. One of my skills is that I can distinguish between people who do and people who pretend to do by exploiting the hard work of others to get to the top of the corporate ladder.

I have a semi-deserved reputation for firing people, a fact I do not deny. I never refer to it as 'firing', however, but rather as 'replacing'. I am the first to admit that I have made some bad appointments, not necessar-ily in terms of skill and talent, but rather in the cultural fit of employees in my organisations. I am not good at interviewing. I'm not sure anyone is, really. Part of the problem is that truly skilful people know how to present themselves in the best light. It is difficult to judge who they really are as people. Even a CV is a poor indicator of whether someone is hard-working or prefers to take it easy. I have always acknowledged that I will make mistakes, which is why I carefully observe new hires in the first couple of months of their employment. This gives me an idea of what each person is capable of, including whether they are hard-working, and whether they are a good fit. Once I know I have made a mistake, I do not waste time. As an entrepreneur with a limited budget, you cannot afford to carry people who can't or won't pull their weight, who are not self-starters and who do not get on with colleagues.

To bring matters to a head, I typically call the person into my office and describe the issue. I tell them that there are two types of successful people: those who thrive in an entrepreneurial environment and those who belong in the corporate world. There is a big difference in personality between the two. The entrepreneurial space is collaborative. We multitask, work hard, celebrate team successes and reward those who deliver. There is no place for corporate hierarchies. In the corporate world, you need to be diplomatic, navigate corporate politics, champion the right people – who, in turn, will pull you up with them – and be generally ruthless. Some people thrive in an entrepreneurial space driven by adrenaline; others are better suited to the 'lone wolf' approach needed to succeed in an established corporate. But you cannot fit a square peg into a round hole. As much as they'd like to, most people will never run their own business. This does not mean they are unsuccessful or unable to achieve their goals. It merely means that different people have different skills and take different paths to success, satisfaction and happiness.

Usually, when I get to the point of having 'a conversation' with an employee, they already know they do not belong. It is, therefore, almost never a surprise or a 'firing'. In most cases, we part ways civilly, mutually recognising that things were just not meant to be. I once employed an incredibly bright actuary who should have been a perfect fit, but for several reasons was not. During our conversation, I compared working for Sygnia with working for Old Mutual. I gave him two weeks to decide which environment would suit him better. I also told him what he would have to do to fit in at Sygnia. A week later, he resigned with a great offer from Old Mutual.

One of my early senior hires loved to boast about the sports cars he owned, including one he had imported for his two-year-old child. He was so disliked by staff that those who were still awake at 3 a.m. during a team-building event took turns leaving messages on his voicemail telling him exactly what they thought of him. It was a brave move that highlighted the type of culture we had developed, one of honesty and no tolerance for one-upmanship. Unsurprisingly, the executive left soon after. Another new senior hire came into my office to ask me how he could make R100 million, as all his friends had already reached that level and he felt he was being left behind. My answer was simple: 'Rob a bank.' He left shortly thereafter, thankfully not taking my advice seriously.

Some of my more notoriously bad senior hires included an actuary who didn't know how to use a basic spreadsheet, a lawyer who had unfortunately lost his eyesight years ago and struggled to read legal documents, a financial director who didn't know how to prepare a budget, and a business development manager whose only desire was to play golf. Some of these were harmless, others more costly.

After five years, we decided to expand beyond Cape Town and set up an office in Johannesburg. While everyone wants to live in the beautiful Mother City, Johannesburg is the business centre of South Africa. Since the start of my career, I had been flying up to Gauteng weekly, sometimes twice a week, so that by the age of thirty-five I had a lifetime gold membership with British Airways. I enjoyed those flights, as they provided a capsule of time in which I could catch up on work uninterrupted by emails and phone calls. I also met interesting people with whom I was able to have uninterrupted conversations for two hours at a time. I never wasted an opportunity to network.

In my Coronation days, I decided to employ someone to assist me with business development, which largely involves setting up meetings, knocking on doors, explaining your products to people who have little time and short attention spans, and generally making a nuisance of yourself. I compare it to being a travelling salesman with a suitcase of watches. My protégé resigned after only a few months, telling me that from the outside what I did looked so glamorous, but from the inside it was grim and soul-destroying.

Business development is the hardest part for any organisation. Like an actor, you can attend hundreds of auditions before winning a part, and every rejection hurts. There are few 'superstars' who get to pick and choose their parts, and Sygnia was certainly no superstar in the beginning. For companies with capital behind them, advertising is sometimes enough to attract clients. I can name several banks, insurance companies and medical schemes in South Africa that were set up on this premise. Investment management businesses are usually lean, with little capital backing them. There is no magic bullet, secret deal or hidden support network when it comes to building up an investment management company, or any honest company for that matter. It takes grit and humility to succeed.

Business development is particularly difficult in a well-established industry dominated by a handful of players. The odds of building a large business in that environment are stacked against you. This is the case not only in South Africa, but also globally. The investment management industry is fragmented into a few dominant brands and a whole host of small boutiques that often do not survive. Apart from sheer tenacity, it also takes time. I have seen several highly skilled investment teams start their own businesses. Many have the potential to grow over time; unfortunately, they are usually bought out the moment a large competitor spots their talent. Tempted by short-term incentives, they end up disappearing into larger corporates, contributing to the narrative that small investment management houses can't thrive.

While many CEOs outsource business development to their juniors, I view it as core to my business and preferred to do it myself. I travelled every week, I set up endless meetings and I sold our story. My trips to Johannesburg were made bearable by my 'second husband', Andrew Steyn, who arrived one day, an uninvited stranger, at our Cape Town offices, knelt on one knee and asked to be employed by Sygnia. After that proposal, who could refuse? Andrew worked at Alexander Forbes in Johannesburg and desperately wanted to join the team I had recently hired. Over the years, he has become a loyal employee and one of my best friends. He thrives in the face of increasing challenges, many of which are forced on him. I've learnt that once you see talent in someone and give them increased responsibility, they tend to outperform your wildest expectations. From his humble beginnings as a client service manager, Andrew now heads up institutional business at Sygnia.

Andrew, my head of retail Trish Jorge and I have taken a few trips overseas together. Once I had to physically support the two highly empathetic people after they broke down on seeing Alcatraz prison in San Francisco. Another trip saw us marching down an empty Fifth Avenue in New York dragging suitcases behind us as we rushed to catch a train. We were there for a Bloomberg conference run alongside a United Nations summit and had not anticipated all the security and dearth of yellow cabs allowed near the Plaza Hotel. I was wearing a designer dress and high heels, having just attended the conference. We looked like a threesome from *Sex in the City*. When we eventually reached a spot where cabs were allowed, no one would stop for a bunch of sweaty people overloaded with luggage. I resorted to waving a fifty-dollar bill at the cabbies before someone eventually took pity on us. We missed the train.

Sygnia was initially criticised by competitors for its perceived key person risk, which arises when a business relies too heavily on one or a small handful of individuals. I was allegedly that key person. This perception was presumably cultivated by our 'on the cheap' marketing strategy, which revolved around me. The reality was very different. In the years since leaving Coronation, where I did everything myself, I had learnt that to grow a successful business you have to delegate. Delegation is difficult when you believe that you can do everything quicker and more efficiently yourself. But there is no scalability in a business model operated by one pair of hands. At the same time, you are not offering others the opportunity to learn and grow. When I finally realised this, my management style evolved into one of delegation and cooperation. For that to work, you need to surround yourself with the right people who share your mindset, core values and, most importantly, have a sense of humour.

15

Ups and Downs

FROM THE OUTSIDE, IT MAY seem that Sygnia's success came easily. But that is an illusion. Everyone worked their fingers to the bone. There was not enough money to spend on support staff, which meant everyone was forced to multitask. I believe that to run a company you need to understand every job in that company. I personally ran the administration of our largest client for several years. It only took an hour each day to perform the various functions, and I did it under the strict supervision of a senior administrator in case I pushed the wrong buttons, but it gave me insight into the progress of the software we were developing and allowed me to find and fix weaknesses and inefficiencies in the processes we were designing.

Not earning salaries and bonuses took a toll on Simon and me. Fortunately, after a few years Sygnia reached the point of being able to pay dividends to its shareholders. As we owned over ninety-five per cent of the shares, that became our reward. I wasn't born into a family that could provide me with easy capital, and I didn't work for a corporate that was willing to back my ideas. I had to forge my own path in the largely white-male-dominated financial services industry, building up a support structure based on individuals rather than departments of technical staff. Frankly, I would not have had it any other way. I'm amused by youngsters in their twenties who dream about becoming instant billionaires on the back of a start-up idea they just had. The vast majority will fail and end up working for large corporates as employees. I prefer to invest in companies where the founders are realistic, in it for the long term and never mention the acronym IPO.

As mentioned previously, the one thing I really enjoyed about building

Sygnia was the independence. There was no one to judge my performance. I was my own harshest critic. There are multiple pressures when you are building a business. There are those you place on yourself, such as knowing that an increasing number of livelihoods depend on your success, and there are external pressures, such as clients expecting a level of service a fledgling business might not be able to deliver. It is important to properly manage these pressures and the stress they create. Some people meditate, others play sports. The treadmill is my preferred stress-management tool.

Sygnia's formative years were joyful. We celebrated every new client by ringing a big brass bell in the boardroom and opening a bottle of champagne for our handful of staff. Over time, as Sygnia grew, we lost some of the original traditions, but not the enthusiasm for building a business. Smaller companies must pay more attention to the well-being and happiness of their staff, because they normally do not have the resources to pay large salaries and bonuses, and depend on people to work harder than they should. To motivate staff, they need to build in other incentives, such as memorable parties, team-building events and even trips overseas.

I love having fun and there is nothing more fun, in my opinion, than Halloween. In the early days of Sygnia, I introduced the tradition of everyone in the office dressing up on Halloween. Everyone would come to work in the morning in their costumes, and at the end of the day we would have a big Halloween-themed party, complete with spooky decor and prizes for the best dressed. I have done everything from painting myself blue to look like a character from *Avatar*, to donning a red wig to transform myself into Poison Ivy. For the first Sygnia Halloween, I went as the Cat in the Hat. I was so well disguised that many staff members did not recognise me. In the afternoon, I had to pick up Nicholas from a school fair, but there was no time to change. As I arrived, I was mobbed by small boys all shouting in excitement, 'Are you the entertainment?' I may have gone all out over the years, but so did everyone else. One year, the investment team had T-shirts made, each labelled with the name of a different well-known investment bank or audit firm allegedly involved in state capture. They all wore black bandannas and eye-masks and carried money bags. Another team dressed up as Snow White and the Seven Dwarves, and another as emojis with yellow-painted faces. Over the years we've had Cabbage Patch Kids, cockroaches, the Joker from *Batman* and Edward Scissorhands. We still have our dress-up tradition, although on a smaller scale nowadays, and the hilarity is just as wild.

I have always placed value on team-building. In the African Harvest days, I gave the entire company an objective: if, through teamwork, we achieved R20 billion in assets under management, I would take everyone to Mauritius. At that stage, we managed around R10 billion, so I was really asking everyone to pull together to double the size of the business. We achieved our objective within a year and I kept my word – we all went to Mauritius. Before leaving, we staged a cocktail party evening to ensure everyone had their fill, as cocktails and alcohol are notoriously expensive in island resorts. This level of extravagance was unheard of in the investment management industry and word got around. The team-build turned out to be a great public relations exercise for us.

At Sygnia, we booked expensive hotels for all team-building events. I don't see the value in long, drawn-out strategy sessions during teambuilds. It is more important for people to bond and have fun, to get to know and like one another. My best team-building experience involved being split up into teams and competing to solve clues to reach a secret destination. Each team was given a minibus and sent on its way. We had to catch hens dyed different colours, ride horses, find bottles in hidden caves on a beach only accessible by scrambling up and down a steep hill, and even compete in archery. These were the days before Google Maps, so you had to rely on actual coordinates and hope that at least one member of your team had some knowledge of navigation. One of my team members claimed to be an expert guide. Where everyone else went left, we went right. Perhaps predictably, we came stone last after a search party was sent to find us. We laughed the entire time.

When Sygnia grew to the point that we had enough executives to have formal executive management team-builds, we introduced overseas trips that married a bit of work with exotic experiences. We decided to change up the group each year, taking all the senior executives but then also selecting different people from different divisions to join us. In that way, we could get to know our staff better and at the same time motivate and thank them for their work. Our first trip was to Dubai. It was probably the least interesting, because Dubai is so artificial. The following year we went to Istanbul, Turkey. Istanbul is a remarkable city, which, apart from its obvious tourist attractions, offers great shopping opportunities if you don't mind counterfeits. The Grand Bazaar is filled with shops selling everything from handbags, shoes and clothing to amulets and spices. I like to negotiate and am not embarrassed by it. At Coronation, the chief executive and head of investments would send me in to negotiate all management fees and contracts on the premise that they were too desperate to get the business to negotiate well. I had less 'skin in the game' and could be more forceful and objective. When I started Sygnia, I was the one with skin in the game and hence overeager. There's skill in knowing when you are not the right person to negotiate. Consequently, I started sending in other people, after giving them strict instructions about the limits they could negotiate around. Over time, they learnt how to negotiate and even where to set the price. Turkey was a good place for us all to practise our skills. I now challenge myself to get the quoted price down by at least fifty per cent. I once spent three days negotiating the price for an old pashmina in India. At the Grand Bazaar, negotiations are expected and welcomed. I soon discovered that if I negotiated hard enough, middlemen would appear out of nowhere. The really good fakes in Istanbul are not sold at the Grand Bazaar, but rather in shops hidden underneath or outside the Bazaar, behind safe doors. It takes some time before the merchants feel comfortable enough to take you to these. The actual team-building in Istanbul was reduced to strategy meetings at eight o'clock every night as everyone wanted to maximise their shopping time. We had so much fun we all went back two years later.

For our last international team-build, just before Covid-19 took hold, we went skiing in France. Out of the eighteen of us, only five could ski.

We hired ski instructors and forced everyone onto bunny slopes. It was a lot of fun and I have never seen so many people rolling around laughing. After a while, as everyone got the hang of it, the skiing turned highly competitive. The experience of learning a new skill had an equalising effect and taught everyone to enjoy one another's company, which usually translates into working well together. We decided to make the skiing team-build a fixture.

I realise that not all businesses can afford such extravagances as overseas trips, and those that can usually restrict them to senior executives. However, I would rather have those experiences with people I like than pay myself bigger dividends or bonuses. At the end of the day, I prefer to create and store memories rather than hoard more money. I don't want to lie on my deathbed and say that I spent all my time working. By marrying work with friendships and memorable experiences, I am able to lead an interesting life.

Sygnia soon outgrew its offices at the V&A Waterfront. It wasn't a large space to begin with, but when boxes of files started to crowd my office, I knew it was time to look for something bigger. I am a reluctant renter. As I have already said, owning property might not be the best investment, but it is a great mechanism for forced saving. As we owned over ninety-five per cent of Sygnia, it made sense to also own all the properties that Sygnia would rent. I had always loved a red-brick building next to a half-finished freeway in Cape Town. It had a different style to many of the surrounding office blocks and was somewhat of an icon. The building, a former chocolate factory repurposed as an advertising agency, was available for rental. I met with the owners and offered to buy the building. They were not interested, but, knowing that the recent global financial crisis was bound to have an impact, I told them to call me when they couldn't find replacement tenants and their banks called in the loans. They phoned me three months later.

I dedicated 2009 and 2010 to my new decorating project. I wanted to create a unique workspace for our staff using art as a starting point, as

Simon and I had become passionate collectors of eclectic art by then. I hired South Africa's most creative interior design and decor studio, Antoni Associates, and instructed them to design an interior that looked more like an art gallery than a traditional office space. My definition of 'art' is broad, spanning architecture, lighting, furniture design, landscaping and the awe-inspiring natural beauty of Cape Town. I sourced light installations from the best international light designers and furniture from South African artists Pierre Cronje, Haldane Martin and Gregor Jenkin. Many of our initial furniture pieces were selected with 'function follows form' in mind. The landscaping took care of itself, as the terrace provided a window onto the extraordinary view of Cape Town city centre, the harbour, Lion's Head and Table Mountain.

We hung all our personal art on the walls. Contemporary art is tricky, with equal numbers of sceptics and supporters, especially in South Africa, where contemporary art has yet to come into its own. In collecting art, Simon and I follow the approach adopted by the founders of Gap, Doris and Donald Fisher. We collect pieces we love with little consideration for the opinions of others. The Fishers' collection, once an eclectic mix of modern art, is now on display in the San Francisco Museum of Modern Art. Our own portfolio, albeit small, is both a passion and an investment. Some pieces are worth little, others will appreciate, and on balance we hope to beat the market. Similar to well-diversified investment strategies, our portfolio is international, featuring artists from South Africa, the US, the UK, Brazil, Australia and Italy. Pieter van der Westhuizen, Ricky Dyaloyi, Jean Doyle and John Meyer sit comfortably alongside Tim Burton, Livio de Marchi, Sarah Graham and Romero Britto. But there is one piece that best reflects Sygnia. Commissioned from David Reade, South Africa's leading glass artist, an installation of over three hundred pieces of hand-blown coloured glass made from sand sourced from the Cape Flats, suspended over two floors, leaves a lasting impression on all our visitors.

We hosted a big party for the grand opening, inviting colleagues, clients, friends, family and even some competitors. 'It is a big night for us,'

I said in my speech. 'We are not only celebrating the opening of our new offices, over which we have shed some real blood and tears, but also the fact that it is the first time we are confident enough to say that Sygnia is a player in the financial services industry in South Africa.'

A few people in my life joined the Sygnia caravan around this time and became stabilising influences. One was Professor Haroon Bhorat, professor of economics and director of the Development Policy Research Unit at UCT. We first met when our sons became best friends in primary school. Several years later I asked him to serve as a chairman of Sygnia. An activist in his youth, Haroon has a pragmatic approach to what is happening in South Africa today. Whenever I have a problem or need someone with a cool head to talk me off a ledge, I phone Haroon. His research has also been extremely valuable to my understanding of the realities of emerging-market economies. He currently serves on Cyril Ramaphosa's Presidential Economic Advisory Panel, and I just wish the government listened to him more.

There was only one minor scandal in those years. In 2012, I received a phone call from a former colleague who told me about a 'novel' penned by a research analyst who worked at Coronation when I was there. I immediately went out and bought the book, which was marketed as a thriller, only to discover that it was based on fact. Everyone who'd worked at Coronation was in the book, including me. In fact, he'd dedicated a whole page to describing my looks. Unsurprisingly, he'd positioned himself as the hero of the story. There was one positive, however. I survived to the end, unlike the head of investments, who was killed by the 'hero' in revenge. It was an appropriate footnote to the Coronation days.

16

The Growth of Sygnia

SYGNIA GREW BEYOND ANYONE'S EXPECTATIONS, and in 2015 we decided to expand our offering by launching products accessible to the person in the street, or, in investment jargon, the retail investor. This is a particularly difficult market to crack without substantial investment in advertising. Most people rely on the advice of their financial advisors, who in turn do not like to take risks on newcomers. If the brand is not widely recognised, they would rather steer their clients to better-known propositions. The administration of a business premised on running thousands of individual accounts was also daunting. Our initial efforts to penetrate the market yielded meagre returns. There was, however, a group of financial advisors, Finsolnet, who did back us initially. Without their support we probably would not have made the decision to launch our unit trust products. They know that I am forever grateful.

We prepared to launch Sygnia's unit trusts on a Monday. On the Friday afternoon before, boxes of thousands of paper application forms arrived on our doorstep. They all had to be captured into the administration system over the weekend. I called the executives together and set them a challenge as to who could load the most applications. Fuelled by an eagerness to win and some pizza, we spent the weekend manually inputting the data. It was important that I was part of the team. I never expect anyone to do anything beyond their scope of responsibilities if I am not prepared to do the same. On Monday, Sygnia's unit trusts were born.

When entering a new fragmented market, it is important to realise that it will be a long and tortuous journey. Any expectation of instant success is a myth. Having said that, I hate starting businesses that are projected to make losses for a long time. I need to clearly see and understand the break-even point. And I prefer that break-even point to be immediate. We hired good operational people, and an amazing sales-person, Trisha, who had no financial services experience but incredible energy and passion. During the two hours in the air on our flights between Cape Town and Johannesburg, she would sit surrounded by dog-eared files, cramming financial concepts into her head and asking a multitude of questions. Today Trisha heads up Sygnia's entire retail division. She is also my sister-in-law, a fact that we did not make public for years as it wasn't relevant to her ability to do the job. Many clients were surprised when they eventually found out.

Trisha is an example of what you can achieve in the workplace through hard work and dedication. It doesn't matter that you do not have the necessary skills or knowledge. Of course, these are helpful, but by themselves they are not enough. I believe that you cannot turn lazy people into hard workers. It doesn't matter what incentives you put on the table. The only thing that will happen if you don't reward hard workers appropriately is that they will leave. I have yet to be proven wrong.

Once again, entering a new market meant we had to innovate. We decided not to charge an administration fee for a lot of our products. It meant we made significantly less profit, but we attracted attention. Given our focus on index tracking investing, we came up with a memorable name for our unit trusts: 'Skeleton' funds. The regulators detest fancy fund names, because, although they create instant recognition, helping with marketing efforts, they say nothing about what the funds actually do. I had to put forward a comprehensive and persuasive argument before the regulators would allow us to use the word 'Skeleton' in our fund names. And it did make the marketing and visual representation of our new funds so much easier. I remember the person who had to sign off on the name telling us that the funds would never sell because death does not go down well with investors. But to us 'Skeleton' was not about death; it was about making things simple, stripping out all the unnecessary costs and offering the fundamentals of the investment product to the consumer.

I have always drawn a distinction between saving and investing. Investing is about deploying money on a short-term basis in the belief, often misguided, that the person doing the investing has some special skill or knowledge about what to invest in to earn significant profits. Saving is about putting money away over the long term and on a regular basis in the most tax-efficient manner possible. It is about a belief in the power of compound interest and time. The tax authorities have designed many products to encourage saving. I use the most tax-efficient products available, such as a retirement annuity and a tax-free savings account, and invest to maximise growth. There are many different assets to choose from, but for average investors, nothing beats listed equities (shares of companies listed on a stock exchange), preferably those outside of an emerging market. Unfortunately, in South Africa there are limits on how much retirement funds and retirement annuities can invest offshore, but those limits should be stretched to the maximum. For savings outside of regulated products, I would always choose offshore investments. Launching Sygnia's retail division allowed me, for the first time in my career, to move away from pure investment management and into offering broader savings products.

Without a large advertising budget, we once again had to turn to cost-effective marketing solutions to boost our retail offering. Fortuitously, by then social media platforms such as Facebook and Twitter had become a lot more popular. I was no stranger to Twitter. By this stage, I had stopped writing opinion pieces, partly because I refused to apologise for the things I wrote and the views I expressed. I needed a new platform to communicate my views, so I turned to Twitter. It is amazing how much you can get across in 280 characters. Today, I mostly use the platform to comment on what I see around me. Some of my commentary triggers journalistic interest, but mostly it's there to air my personal views and occasionally to educate people. I also use Twitter to ensure that events in South Africa, particularly those involving corruption, are not swept under the carpet. I try to keep my political views to myself and remain impartial. I try not to impose my beliefs on others. Twitter can be an unforgiving medium and has landed me in hot water in the past. My worst mistake was incorrectly posting a photo of Hector Pieterson to commemorate the Sharpeville massacre, when of course he was a victim of the Soweto uprising in June 1976. It took me exactly a minute to realise my mistake and delete the tweet. But that minute was enough. A simple mistake is instantly and, I suspect, automatically screen-grabbed and retweeted faster than you can hit the delete button. Some of my comments, although well meaning, have been twisted and distorted – the disadvantage of 280 characters – and I have been the target of malicious Twitter bots. The only subject about which I have not been able to remain impartial is Covid-19 vaccinations. I believe that the vaccines have made a significant difference, and I was first in line when I qualified for one. As much as I disagree with the economic lockdowns, the protection of the vulnerable was difficult to achieve in the initial stages of the pandemic. But the development of the vaccines changed that. I don't think I'll ever understand the anti-vaxxer movement.

Back in 2015, our marketing department took to social media like ducks to water. Advertising was cheap to create and could be distributed to exactly the right target market. Our global marketing consultant, my sister, Ashka, who had many years of film production experience behind her name, made our adverts herself to keep costs to a minimum. We wanted our adverts to be relevant to people's lives. We cut the jargon and tried to make investment concepts uncomplicated and accessible. Investment education using social media channels has proved to be the perfect formula. Most of our advertising on Facebook and Twitter now focuses on investor education.

Social media spread our message far and wide, and suddenly Sygnia was a brand in the retail market. This brought its own set of challenges, but we were proud of what we'd achieved. Through innovation, we had harnessed an evolving technology and built our advertising strategy around it. Other investment managers are only now waking up to what we've been doing all along. Now they are imitators without a first-mover advantage. To my mind, print advertising and billboards especially are becoming obsolete. How much money was wasted on billboards at empty airports during the Covid-19 pandemic? Our strategy means that we did not spend money on something irrelevant, and that may remain irrelevant for years to come. Social media platforms have become critical in a world of low attention spans. Used wisely, they can influence opinion and educate, but used maliciously, they spread fake news. I am cautious of what I see on social media. If it is a topic that interests me, I try to verify the information with other sources. I do not take anything at face value.

While we were building our retail offering, another exciting development was brewing. In 2013, we had decided that Sygnia was ready for a listing on the JSE. It took us two years to achieve, but we had a clear goal. Prior to making the decision, we had a strategy session in Dubai to debate the merits of the idea. There was so little to do in Dubai that I could get everyone around the table for a real strategy session, undistracted by emails and other demands on their time. We left with a common understanding that it would be advantageous in the long run. Apart from the possibility of raising capital should we wish to make acquisitions, listing would give us a much higher level of recognition in the industry. Being listed offers you endless opportunities for free publicity. Newspapers are more inclined to write about listed companies than private ones.

I consider myself extremely lucky to have had the opportunity to list a company on a stock exchange. It is normally a once-in-a-lifetime experience that brings with it both extreme highs and extreme lows. The first thing I learnt about listing on the JSE is that it is a very expensive process. The costs originate from multiple sources, including having to appoint sponsors, advisors, lawyers and auditors. Negotiating the fees to a reasonable, preferably capped, level is key. I looked at the pre-listing statements of other listed companies to get an idea of what I should be paying and to whom. Looking at it objectively, the auditors undoubtedly do most of the work and deserve the rewards. Their relative contribution is followed by that of the sponsors, who act as the link between the stock exchange and the company. Lawyers also deserve their spot in the sun, although I would beware of any fee structures that involve hourly rates.

Advisors, in my opinion, come last. Apart from general advice, which tends to overlap with the role of the sponsors, they are responsible for introducing the company to institutional investors, such as investment managers, hedge funds and wealth managers. This enables them to charge a hefty percentage of the capital raised at listing as their fee. The sums payable to advisors become astronomical very quickly.

From an advisory perspective, the best advice I received came from canvassing the opinions of a wide range of people who had been involved in the listing process in the past. The stock exchange itself also helped us. Once we had canvassed, we decided that we didn't need advisors. We could make our own appointments with institutional investors, deliver our own marketing presentations and listen carefully to whatever feedback we received. That said, we were lucky in that we knew the investment management industry well. If I was listing a construction business, I might be more willing to pay for introductions, which is really all that capital raising entails. I remember presenting to the investment management division of one of the largest life insurance companies in the country. Given my love affair with branding and design, our presentation was very colourful and eye-catching. After my pitch, in which I explained the merits of investing in Sygnia, I opened the floor to questions. There was only one. A dinosaur of the industry asked whether we expected to raise any money with 'those slides'. It reminded me of the early days at Alexander Forbes, something about grey-suited men in brown shoes. Needless to say, their investment division is not highly rated in the market.

The Sygnia Limited listing was 19.8 times oversubscribed, which meant that we only had enough shares to allocate to one in almost twenty people who wanted to buy them. Some called it a huge success; others were deeply critical of the small or no allocations they received. In truth, behind the scenes, the numbers were completely overwhelming, with R5.2 billion chasing R262 million in share placement. There is no ideal way to deal with oversubscription. The lesson I learnt is that it is key to decide on the rules of the game ahead of time and stick to them, irrespective of pressure to do otherwise. That pressure cannot be underestimated. It is amazing what people will do when faced with the prospect of easy 'staging' money.

That is when you buy shares at the listing price on the day of the actual listing, in expectation that the price will shoot up, and then immediately sell them when it does. When making allocations, you are the person standing between people and cash. Threats, screaming and verbal abuse were commonplace in the three days leading up to the listing. We had the option of choosing our investors, and we made a lot of mistakes. We naturally made allocations to friends, family and clients, and having credible investment managers on the share register was also helpful. But we also allocated shares to a few entities that we lived to regret. It was a case of not doing enough due diligence ahead of the process. What makes share issues complicated is that you have exactly one afternoon between the close of the offer period and issuing communication to finalise the allocations.

The day of the listing found the entire executive management team of Sygnia and my family in Johannesburg for a morning function at the JSE. There was excitement in the air. For good luck, I had chosen to list the company on 14 October, my birthday. The executive team of the JSE prepared a large birthday cake for me, and I got to celebrate two events on the same date. Listing in Johannesburg does not involve ringing a bell, as it does at the New York Stock Exchange. Instead, you blow a large kudu horn. It is so heavy that you need help holding it up. You also receive training in how to blow it ahead of the actual event. I blew the horn just as the market opened, and we watched the board in amazement and disbelief as the share price of Sygnia skyrocketed.

Sygnia's 2015 listing has been a mixed blessing. While it has generated a higher profile for the company, with many clients deriving comfort from investing with a listed entity, and has enabled us to raise capital to make an acquisition, listing has come with many disadvantages. The need to explain your financial results biannually to research analysts working for competitors and to investors means that all your affairs and strategies are transparent. For a company like Sygnia, which likes to operate by stealth in terms of new strategies, it is deeply uncomfortable. Our listing also came at an unfortunate time, as small companies such as Sygnia were abandoned by institutional investors who increasingly focused on large corporates in terms of their investment strategies.

Our listing coincided with the South African economy entering a downwards spiral. Opportunities for making smart acquisitions simply disappeared. There were a few overpriced businesses with poor business strategies, but nothing particularly attractive. I was also acutely aware of the difficulties of integrating different companies, people and cultures, and how it demands time away from core activities.

The publicity associated with being a listed company is a double-edged sword. Everything we do, no matter how insignificant, must be announced on a public wire service. It is sometimes difficult to keep track of all the JSE rules relating to actions that require such announcements, and the announcements themselves often give rise to interpretative journalism, short on facts and big on sensational headlines, which I then have to explain. It is this kind of thing that makes Sygnia easy prey for competitors who resent our success. Personally, I have never committed to Sygnia being my last business venture. I believe in branching out and doing other things. But any whiff of this tends to generate headlines. On one occasion, Simon and I had to do some financial restructuring whereby I transferred some Sygnia shares into his name. We were required to make a public announcement about it and the newspapers immediately picked up the 'story'. A journalist contacted me to get the details. Although the explanation was innocuous, he ran an article with the headline 'Sygnia CEO Magda Wierzycka donates R216m worth of shares to her spouse'. He phoned me that afternoon to joyfully tell me that his story had generated the most clicks of any article published that day. It soon led to rumours that Simon and I had divorced. Despite denials from us, our family and friends, the rumours wouldn't go away. I eventually used Twitter and a radio interview to set things straight.

For anyone contemplating a listing on a stock exchange, you need to carefully examine why this is your objective. If it is merely to validate the value of your investment in the company, and thus your net worth, I would immediately discard the idea. If it is to sell some of your shares, this does not normally go down well with other investors. It is better to find investors invisibly while remaining unlisted. Some small companies have abandoned their listings in recent years, delisting from the stock exchange. Sygnia is too large to do so easily.

17

Taking Sygnia into the Future

I N 2016, DURING A TRIP to Los Angeles to attend a conference on
innovation, I was introduced to the concept of the Fourth Industrial
Revolution, defined as new technologies merging the physical and digital
worlds. The scope and speed of the breakthroughs are astounding. They
are already disrupting almost every sphere of life as we know it, at a much
quicker pace than we expected. We are seeing innovations in drone
technology, self-driving and electric vehicles, robotics, virtual reality,
3D printing, clean energy, genetic engineering, artificial intelligence, new
payment methods, healthcare provision and space exploration. In 2021
alone, novel vaccines based on new technologies reached billions of
people in the shortest time ever in pharmaceutical development. Space
exploration moved beyond a rover on Mars, as the year saw the launch of
the James Webb Space Telescope and the first 'space tourism', now offered
by several private companies. Artificial intelligence is making a real impact
on drug research. Progress in the application of quantum computing to
real-world problems continues exponentially, with Google's 'quantum
supremacy' experiment surpassed by six orders of magnitude. (Quantum
supremacy is the long sought-after proof that a computer built around
quantum mechanics can carry out calculations exponentially faster than a
classical computer.) It is a sign of the times that Elon Musk, the genius
behind Tesla, SpaceX and The Boring Company, was named as *Time* magazine's Person of the Year for 2021. As most people know, Musk is a South
African who left the country when he was a teenager.

Living on the southern tip of Africa, it's easy to miss what's happening
in the world. I think for many of us, South Africa is a comfortable bubble,
particularly if you learn to ignore the country's political and economic

troubles. Even with all my travelling, I've realised that I, too, focus too much on the past and not enough on the future.

The conference in LA was an eye-opener. I drove an electricity-powered Tesla with self-driving features. I played a virtual reality game. I saw talking and walking robots and a 3D-printed house. I walked away convinced of the investment potential of all these ideas, as future investment returns are likely to be generated by companies that embrace and focus on these new technologies. Large industrial corporates as we know them are slowly becoming sunset industries from an investment perspective.

At almost the same time, my younger son was on a school exchange programme in Pittsburgh in the United States, a city chosen to test self-driving Ubers. With some trepidation I got to go in one. It was early days and a number of 'kinks' around safety still required working out, but it was a glimpse of the future. I also saw Amazon drones doing test deliveries. And at Sygnia, the software development team became obsessed with the beta version of Oculus Rift, the virtual reality headsets used for gaming. There was a lot of excitement as everyone tried to play the then rudimentary games without becoming nauseous. Renewable energy had also started to become a hot topic in providing a partial solution to the rapid progress of climate change.

I immediately began looking for ways to benefit from my newfound knowledge and expose our clients to it. As an index tracking investment manager, the optimal solution was to find someone who had already scoured the global markets for such companies and compiled an appropriate index for us to replicate in terms of actual investments made. I found a start-up in New York called Kensho which was doing just that. I got on the next flight to the US, met with them and signed exclusive rights to use their indices in South Africa.

In November 2016, we launched what is still the most innovative product in the market, the Sygnia 4th Industrial Revolution Global Equity Fund, which offers South African investors exposure to global companies at the forefront of driving the Fourth Industrial Revolution. I remember doing all the initial marketing presentations to the general bemusement and amazement of my audiences. The fund was a huge hit from the start. Once again, innovation rather than imitation worked for Sygnia in spectacular fashion, and the product and the presentations firmly positioned us as a market disruptor.

But a disruptor cannot stop. My latest obsession is the Metaverse, a digital world where your virtual self, or avatar, can shop for clothes or cars, buy property, go to concerts and socialise with others. All you need is a VR headset, a microphone, handheld consoles and some cryptocurrency to immerse yourself in an alternate reality. As much as the appeal may be limited to Millennials and Gen Z, it offers limitless marketing and sales opportunities for companies brave enough to enter that world early. Once again, Sygnia is launching a product that invests in companies which should benefit from the emergence of the Metaverse at a time when most people have never heard of the concept.

Given my experiences selling African Harvest, I thought my next corporate transaction would be a cinch. I was wrong.

In 2017, Deutsche Bank put db X-trackers (DBX), their exchange traded fund business, up for sale. Exchange traded funds are just index tracking unit trusts that are listed on a stock exchange. Whereas you can only invest in a normal unit trust once a day, you can buy and sell exchange traded funds throughout the day as if they are shares in a company.

On the surface, the structure of DBX was very simple. It was a 'business in a box' with one employee. Everything was outsourced. It was a deeply attractive proposition, and so, unsurprisingly, most financial services companies were in the running. As a relatively small company, Sygnia could hardly compete with the much deeper wallets of some of our competitors. We had one advantage, however – in-depth knowledge of all the different pieces of legislation that applied to a company of that nature. We soon realised that DBX's legal structure contravened existing South African financial regulations set by National Treasury.

Somehow, despite competing with boardrooms full of lawyers, we were the only ones to spot this significant problem. Deutsche Bank assured me they had all the necessary permissions to implement the transaction, but I knew better and simply sat back and waited.

Sygnia was not the highest bidder for the business, but, in the end, an embarrassed Deutsche Bank executive approached us, admitting that we were right and asking us to help legitimise the structure. I came up with a very complex corporate transaction that would have satisfied the regulators, but our arguments were sufficiently persuasive that National Treasury amended their regulations and Sygnia got DBX at a good price. This was the first and last time we used our JSE listing to raise money for an acquisition.

The lessons of my youth had served me well. Armed with legal knowledge acquired over many years, and not relying on lawyers and corporate advisors, I could easily spot what others had missed. Had I passed on the opportunities to learn and just focused on climbing the corporate ladder, I would never have achieved what I did. This is a good example of how one person's determination can move mountains, or at least change legislation for the better.

I have waged various legislative wars in my career, always on the side of the consumer. I have lost a lot of them, but I always hope that when regulators read my forty-page policy proposals they may change their minds. Whether my proposals actually get read or just end up in the dustbin, who knows. Either way, I like writing them. They force you to research and analyse, clarify your thinking and put together logical arguments, whether you're writing a policy proposal addressing regulation or a business proposal to put forward to your manager.

Unfortunately, 2017 was also the year I fell in love with bitcoin and gave in to 'tulip mania'. Tulip mania took hold of the Netherlands in the 1600s and is widely viewed as the first financial asset bubble. I initially made a lot of money and then, in a flash, lost it all and then some. Even the most seasoned investment managers can make mistakes when seduced by easy linear returns. It was an education in impulsive behaviour, and I have since become a lot more cautious. Unless you have researched the asset, do not be swayed by popular opinion. The only positive takeaway from the whole experience was that I learnt a lot about blockchain technology. And clearly, if I'd held on and had more patience and less fear, I would have made a lot of money again by 2021.

I have also changed my views about the merit of investing in hedge funds over the years. A hedge fund is essentially an investment fund that promises not to lose your money in exchange for you giving up some of the upside returns. They're a great proposition to people like me, who prefer to protect their wealth rather than risk losing it through the vagaries of the investment markets. When I left Coronation and started IQvest in 2003, the first product we launched was a fund of hedge funds. At the time, I was a great believer in hedge funds and invested most of my own savings in them. However, what initially held great promise over time became nothing more than a money-making racket for hedge fund managers. The promise of protection never materialised, despite the funds' substandard performance relative to normal investment products. The management fees became obscene against the backdrop of mediocre returns. Even today, there are hedge funds that barely outperform cash in the bank and yet are charging close to ten per cent per annum in management and performance-based fees. In 2018, we decided to close the product offering and return all the money to the investors. We informed our clients of the closure, and I wrote an article for a leading business publication motivating our decision and highlighting the extraordinary fees charged by hedge fund managers. There was a general outcry from both investors, who only then realised the fees they had been paying, and hedge fund managers, whose lucrative livelihoods were threatened by the exposure. To this day, many still view me as an enemy.

This decision cost us a significant revenue stream, but we believed it was the right thing to do.

18

Does Money Motivate?

'DOES MONEY MOTIVATE?' was an essay question in one of the first courses I took at university, called Management of Human Resources. The course was run by a cranky professor who had a reputation for being extremely tough on students. The essay constituted a large percentage of our final mark for the course and I spent the Easter break researching the topic in depth. In the pre-internet days this meant sitting in dusty libraries, pulling random books off the shelves and hoping to gain some insights. In the end, I got the highest mark for my efforts and even went on to win the class medal for the course.

I've had reason to ponder that question over the years. Given our background, my siblings and I have a complicated relationship with money. We grew up under communism, where, for the most part, everyone had just enough but everyone had the same – the same apartment, the same tiny car, the same religious holidays, the same presents, the same everything. As modest as our existence was relative to children in the West, we wanted for nothing. When we escaped Poland, we left everything behind, from all our family photos to my Lego blocks and my favourite pair of red shoes. I have forgiven my parents for most things, but not for making me leave those red shoes. When we lived in the refugee camp and subsequently in the guesthouse in Austria, we had nothing and were treated as such. As I have already mentioned, my father dug ditches in the middle of winter to make some money for us to spend on Western luxuries such as yoghurt in the local supermarket. We used cardboard boxes as makeshift sledges while Austrian children had fancy wooden ones. When we arrived in South Africa, my parents had five hundred US dollars in cash. That was all. But unlike many impoverished South Africans, we had two advantages: my parents both had stable, albeit low-paying jobs, and my siblings and I had a strong foundation in education.

Having nothing but my skill set meant that I attached very little value to personal possessions. Not much has changed. The truth is I could leave it all behind and start again. The prospect really does not scare me. Consequently, I have never been motivated by money. Achieving success is motivation enough. To me success means being able to look at myself in the mirror every morning and saying, 'I am pleased with who I am, I have friends, I have a loving family, and I am trying to make a difference in society.' Money is not the goal, it is merely the enabler; it enables me to live the life I want, to help my family, and others, when required, to ensure my children receive the best possible education, to go on adventure holidays, and to retire in comfort one day.

The money I have made over the years has come from my own hard work. I was never going to inherit anything. I knew from an early age that I had to make my own way in life and that other people would depend on me financially. So, as much as money is not a motivator, I also could not walk away from money in my early years. It is part of the reason I did not find it easy to leave Coronation.

In 2018, I was invited to talk about money on a prominent radio talk show. The questions I was sent ahead of time revolved around the subject of making money. One was: How much money is enough? The truth is that 'enough' is different for different people. For most of us, enough means the ability to buy a nice house, educate our children, live comfortably and retire in the knowledge that we are financially secure. Few people realistically strive to own private jets, yachts and luxury cars. Most are happy with a modest life, as long as it is a happy and healthy one. As much as I have enjoyed some of the luxuries that come with making money, such as the ability to travel and buy Aston Martins, making money has come at a heavy cost – of always working, even during 'holidays', time spent away from my family, the pressure of being responsible for livelihoods of staff and the stress of dealing with unhappy clients, which I take very personally. Deducting that cost from the money I have in the bank would leave me with very little.

Another question was what excites me about money. When I thought more deeply about it, I realised that nothing about money excites me. Making a difference and a contribution excites me, as does leading an interesting and sometimes entertaining life. Money by itself has little meaning. What scares me most isn't losing the money I have made, but getting older and losing some of the energy to power ahead. Ageing is inevitable, but I do wish I was ten years younger.

If money is all that you seek in life, and the only thing that gives you validation, yours will be a sad existence. At the end of the day, there is only so much you can spend. I can only buy so many pairs of shoes or handbags, and my husband already complains about the handbags. At some point, you will have made enough. At that point, you need to think about what it is that gives you true validation and how you can make a difference, even if only on a small scale. For all their horror, the KwaZulu-Natal and Gauteng riots of July 2021 brought divergent communities together. I would guess that, after the dust settled, all those people who banded together to protect property from looters remember those days as the most meaningful of their lives. It was not a pay cheque that gave them validation and motivation. It was a sense of common purpose.

Money also influences friendships. In my experience, it is difficult to make friends when you have a lot of money. You may be surrounded by people, but you can never be sure whether they're there because they enjoy your company, or because they want something from you. Being in the public eye has also meant that my trust levels are a lot lower than they used to be. When it comes to friendships, and based on a few bad experiences, I tend to surround myself with people I knew before I became wealthy, people who were there in the early days, who liked me for who I was and not for what I became.

My brother and sister have a similar approach to money, although, as I've mentioned, they are both more conservative than me. My sister is always sending me the latest budgeting app that she's using, and it took my brother over forty years to buy his first house. That said, the three of us are still sitting on suitcases, ready to pick them up, move and start over if needs be.

19

The Scourge of Corruption

WITH MY KNOWLEDGE OF FINANCE and my interest in crime shows and crime fiction, I have always been particularly fascinated – and appalled – by white-collar financial crime. I believe it takes a particular psychopathy to plan and perpetrate a fraud that strips victims of their livelihood. Financial crimes are also notoriously difficult to prosecute due to their complexity. Perhaps my fascination with the topic is one of the reasons I became an anti-corruption 'activist'.

In 2007, one of the largest financial crimes in South Africa came to light. It involved a little-known company called Fidentia, run by J. Arthur Brown. I had met his partner in crime, Graham Maddock, when I was at African Harvest. Maddock had tried to sell me their administration services. Between the two, they managed to get hold of the Living Hands Umbrella Trust, a provident fund for about fifty thousand widows and orphans of mineworkers. Between 2002 and 2006, they plundered its assets and splurged on luxury offices, sports clubs, a pole-dancing operation and even a spa. Brown was first arrested in 2007. Out of curiosity, Simon and I attended his bail hearing. I thought we'd be able to sneak into the courtroom unnoticed, but I was unfamiliar with the layout of a South African magistrate's court. As we opened the door, we came face to face with Brown himself. Literally. The lectern from which he was testifying was positioned right next to the door, and the proceedings were already under way. The room was tiny, with just enough space for the magistrate, the lawyers and a handful of observers perched on a small bench pressed against the back wall. When we entered, everyone stopped. As it was too late to make a dignified retreat, we shuffled, embarrassed, to the bench and sat down.

Brown gave quite a performance. At one point, his lawyer tried to intervene, but was rebuffed by his own client. Brown told a colourful story about Fidentia and his accountability, or lack thereof, but it soon became clear that when it comes to white-collar crime, it is difficult for prosecutors who typically do not have the requisite financial knowledge to know what questions to ask to distinguish truth from lies. I had to resist the impulse to stand up and take over the questioning. A very smart senior counsel once told me that the best way to prosecute white-collar crime is to go after one simple crime to prove misdeed. Just one. I call it the 'stolen pencil theory'. If one can prove, beyond any doubt, that a simple crime has been committed, there is little room to appeal and the perpetrator will likely go to jail. More complex charges can be brought later.

South Africa has a robust legal framework around asset freezing and forfeiture when a crime is suspected. This prevents the accused from spending their potentially ill-gotten gains on their own defence or, worse still, hiding it. After several court battles, and thanks to the persistence of South African regulators, Brown was ultimately sentenced to fifteen years in prison in 2014, but that was of little comfort to his victims. Only a quarter of the R1.3 billion was ever recovered by the curators. A few years later, the head of a large trade union told me about the heartbreaking consequences for the widows deprived of their livelihoods. Forced into abject poverty, they were not able to educate their children, many of whom turned to drugs and crime. No one came to their aid.

My own first brush with corruption came in the African Harvest days. One of our clients was a large government-linked retirement fund. When it came time for the annual review of all their investment manager appointments, I was invited to lunch by three members of the board of trustees responsible for managing the fund's affairs. They unashamedly asked me how much I was willing to pay to keep the appointment, as 'everyone else was paying them'. I told them: 'Gentlemen, I am prepared to pay for the lunch.' We lost the client. I brought this up with the fund's management, but it appeared they were aware of the issue and were not prepared to do anything about it.

My second encounter came in the early days of Sygnia. At the time, we had, again, one very large, government-linked insurance fund as a client that was material to our financials. Two years into our appointment, the board responsible for overseeing the fund changed. The new chairperson set up a meeting with me and proposed that Sygnia double its fee and pay the difference over to her. I refused. Clearly confused, she felt she had to explain that Sygnia would not be worse off through the arrangement. When I still refused, she threatened to take the business away. I remained unmoved, and she kept her word. I consulted lawyers at the time about bringing her to account but was told that as there was nothing in writing, it was her word against mine. Many years later, I was approached by investigators to provide an affidavit as to what happened when Sygnia was unexpectedly replaced as the fund's investment manager. I thought the wheels of justice might be turning, but she remains on the board to this day.

In another incident in the early days of Sygnia, an investment consultancy approached us claiming that a client we had recently acquired had requested their services. We soon learnt that this was not the case. It turned out this consultancy mostly appointed investment managers to manage their clients' assets if the investment managers were willing to pay for a range of superficial services provided by the investment consultancy. The services were of little value and were really a means of channelling a portion of management fees paid by clients to investment managers back to the consultancy. When confronted, they merely said, 'You have to pay to play.' We fired them, but they continue to operate in this manner today.

I never cared when I lost assets or did not get new business premised on dishonesty. You cannot place a price on your integrity.

Dishonesty and greed are not limited to the financial services industry. Corruption became deeply entrenched in the South African government, particularly after Jacob Zuma became president of the country in 2009. The ANC's former head of espionage and counter-intelligence may not have a formal education, but he has been described to me by people who spent time with him on Robben Island as being incredibly shrewd.

When Zuma outsmarted Thabo Mbeki to become the president of the ANC at the party's national conference in Polokwane in 2007, Mzi Khumalo, who was still a powerful force within its ranks, phoned me. He had just left the conference and he was furious. I will never forget his words. 'Magda,' he said, 'a gallery of rogues has taken over my ANC.' I am still amazed at how prophetic that turned out to be. He clearly was not referring to everyone in the party, but those who subsequently tried to stop Zuma were promptly replaced.

Zuma's brushes with the law are infamous, but no account of his alleged crimes would be complete without saluting Fezekile Ntsukela Kuzwayo, initially known to the South African public only as Khwezi to protect her identity. She was the daughter of Judson Kuzwayo, an ANC veteran who had spent ten years on Robben Island with Zuma. In 2005, she courageously accused Zuma, then the deputy president of the ANC, of rape. When she passed away in 2016 at the age of forty-one, the former minister of intelligence services and friend of the family, Ronnie Kasrils, was quoted in the press as saying: 'We should never forget her name. Fezeka Kuzwayo. Her life was completely smashed in 2005 and 2006. She was abused, hounded and castigated. It broke her. Her house was burnt down. She stood as a symbol for all of us who are abused in this violent, disgusting and patriarchal way. She is an example of what we must not do. We must show solidarity with those who are vilified for speaking out.'

Zuma was acquitted of the rape charge in 2006, after claiming that the sex had been consensual and that he 'took a shower' to prevent becoming infected with HIV/AIDS.

By then he had also been indirectly accused of taking bribes from French company Thomson-CSF (now Thales) in South Africa's multibillion-rand arms deal. The bribes were allegedly solicited by his financial advisor, Schabir Shaik. In 2005, Shaik was found guilty of corruption and fraud by the KwaZulu-Natal High Court for paying Zuma R1.2 million to 'further their relationship', for soliciting a bribe from Thales, and for writing off more than R1 million of Zuma's unpaid debts. In 2009, after serving just over two years of his fifteen-year prison sentence, Shaik was released on medical parole on the grounds that he had an incurable ailment and wanted a dignified death. More than a decade later, he is still alive and seemingly doing well.

Zuma's ascension to power came soon after the global financial crisis of 2007–2008, which saw stock markets crash on the back of the financial services industry's greed. Banks around the world incurred huge losses and relied on government support to avoid bankruptcy. That support came in the form of massive stimulus packages, including reducing interest rates to almost zero, printing money to stimulate borrowing and spending, and buying illiquid and potentially worthless assets from banks to provide them with liquidity. 'Too big to fail' became the catchphrase.

This meant that the same opportunistic players, now liquid again, were able to borrow money at near zero interest rates and invest it in markets that offered higher interest rates and returns. It was a huge, almost riskless, arbitrage opportunity. South Africa was paying higher interest rates on any money it borrowed due to the perceived risk of the country defaulting on the obligation to repay its debts. If the economy had been stronger and better managed, and the government had more international credibility, the rates would have been lower and the money saved could have been diverted to more worthy causes, such as education, healthcare, infrastructure and other basic services. Unfortunately, the government's inability to implement economic policies to boost growth and employment took its toll. Consequently, due to the attractive returns on offer, foreign investors were more than willing to lend South Africa money and invest in corporates listed on the JSE. The inflow of all this artificial 'hot' money created a perception of prosperity in the country, as savings grew on paper and people thought they were getting wealthier.

Nothing could have been further from the truth, but no one was paying attention.

In the decade under Zuma, the country became even poorer, crime skyrocketed, infrastructure started failing and unemployment rose. No one noticed the enormity of the crisis. It happened incrementally, by virtue of the actions of people who, until 2016, remained in the shadows. Until then, few people recognised the name 'Gupta'; fewer still knew that they were three brothers with a close relationship to Jacob Zuma. Those who were paying attention only knew that they had somehow managed to land private aeroplanes full of wedding guests from India at Air Force Base Waterkloof back in 2013. The wedding was obscene in its decadence and shrouded in secrecy due to strict security measures employed by the Guptas, but a few details did leak out and were even covered by the media. However, most South Africans remained largely oblivious to both the excess and the fact that we were paying for it.

The first public clue to what later became known as 'state capture' came in December 2015, when Zuma fired finance minister Nhlanhla Nene and replaced him with the little-known Des van Rooyen in what was widely seen as an attempt at gaining complete control over South Africa's purse strings. After a massive public backlash, and a sharp fall in the value of the rand, the four days' wonder, Van Rooyen, was replaced by the well-respected Pravin Gordhan. Unfortunately, Van Rooyen's tenure, however short-lived, was not without consequences. He is alleged to have passed sensitive government plans meant for the cabinet to the Guptas' lieutenants and has emerged as one of the major figures in the allegations of state capture.

In early 2016, deputy finance minister Mcebisi Jonas issued a statement revealing that, before Van Rooyen's appointment, the Guptas had offered the job of finance minister to him, provided he toed their line. In fact, Jonas stated that one of the Gupta brothers, Ajay, threatened to kill him if he ever mentioned this or the R600-million bribe he was offered and refused. In another revelation, ANC member of Parliament Vytjie Mentor claimed that back in 2010 the Guptas had offered her the post of minister of public enterprises, replacing Barbara Hogan, if she dropped SAA's lucrative flight route between Johannesburg and Mumbai in favour of an Indian airline, Jet Airways, in which the Guptas had a stake. And Barbara Hogan confirmed that she had been pressured by the Guptas to meet with their nominated airline in 2010, while she had still been public enterprises minister.

The Guptas' name started to appear more and more among growing allegations of misuse of public funds, illegal procurement processes, corruption of government officials and mismanagement of state-owned enterprises (SOEs) such as Eskom, Denel and Transnet.

Subsequent evidence has made it clear that many people participated in the heist, from cabinet ministers to boards of directors and managers of SOEs, as well as senior figures in government departments. There seems to have been no limit to the plunder that took place, and that unfortunately continues to this day. Zuma knew that to hide his own actions he had to enable and encourage others to do the same. Together with the Guptas, he institutionalised dishonesty across the public and private sectors and hijacked the state. It was astonishingly easy. All he had to do was dismantle the National Prosecuting Authority (NPA) and its priority crime investigation unit, the Scorpions, and the South African Revenue Service (SARS), which is responsible for tax collection. Whoever stood in his way was replaced. Zuma reshuffled his cabinet an incredible eleven times. Thankfully, he failed to capture and destroy the South African Reserve Bank and National Treasury. The Reserve Bank managed to retain its independence due largely to its governor, Lesetja Kganyago, who has resisted all attempts at subverting the institution. Treasury was saved largely thanks to Mcebisi Jonas, for his refusal of the R600-million bribe to enable the Guptas to take over Treasury. Had Zuma succeeded, South Africa as we know it would not exist today. We are privileged to have Mcebisi on Sygnia's board of directors today.

20

Taking a Stand

Life is full of choices. You choose whether to be guided by your moral compass or not. You choose to make a real difference or you don't. When I talk about making a difference, I don't mean impersonally or indirectly. Writing a cheque, employing more staff than you need, even building a business that creates jobs are relatively easy things to do in a country such as South Africa. The law even dictates that each corporate must spend money on socially responsible investments. Although all the above are important and do make a contribution, when I talk about making a difference, I mean personally and directly taking action that impacts people's lives. Not many people think in these terms, and that's fine. The world needs the entrepreneurs and managers who start and run successful businesses that create jobs and contribute to the economy, but it also needs a few fearless or reckless idealists who are willing to take risks. I am not sure how I found myself in the latter category, but once I took one step, another one followed, and then came a point when there was no turning back. Perhaps it's my childhood, or my family's history, but I have a thirst for justice, even when I know I am tilting at windmills.

My first activist crusade was in early 2017 when I stumbled on an article about a little-known company called Net1 Universal Electronic Payment System (UEPS) Technologies, which was supported by one of the largest investment managers in South Africa. Something in the article triggered my interest and my suspicion. I took a weekend off to do some sleuthing. Sitting on my couch, I searched every corner of the internet for information about Net1. From analysts' interviews to Securities and Exchange Commission (SEC) filings, the story began to unfold. The company turned out to be a bit like an onion – every time I peeled away a layer, I uncovered something else. Net1 and its subsidiary, Cash Paymaster Services (CPS), had been appointed to distribute social grants through a dodgy tender process run by the South African Social Security Agency (SASSA) that was declared invalid by the Constitutional Court in 2014. SASSA was given until March 2017 to find an alternative, although this was extended to 2018 by the court. The grants were paid into bank accounts registered in each grant recipient's name and held by a small bank. Each grant recipient was issued with a credit card. The social grants were paid monthly, but only once recipients had verified their identity via a voice call or through fingerprints taken at any qualifying pay point or store. This resulted in long queues of the poorest of the poor. CPS used the queuing system to market micro-loans, life insurance products, airtime and prepaid electricity to the waiting people, siphoning off the payments for these products directly from the recipients' bank accounts.

There are over seventeen million grant recipients in South Africa. By December 2016, Net1 had 142 branches, 936 ATMs and 1895 dedicated sales staff selling 'financial services' to people who could hardly afford to keep roofs over their heads. Most alarmingly, Net1 charged an effective annual interest rate of 164 per cent for long-term loans and 280 per cent for short-term loans. As they deducted the repayments directly from the grant amounts, which were guaranteed by the government, they were never at any risk of non-payment. An interest rate of prime plus two per cent would have been more appropriate. It was exploitation, pure and simple. Net1 was listed on the Nasdaq and the JSE. It was not a small company that could fly under the radar. At its peak in 2017 it was worth over R9 billion. To this day, I cannot believe that active investment managers propped up Net1, and even crowed about it being a successful investment. It took me a weekend to uncover the truth. They had teams of research analysts whose full-time job it was to analyse Net1. How could they not know? And if they did, how could they not care?

Driven by a sense of indignation, I wrote a series of articles detailing my discovery and published them in an independent newspaper. All hell broke loose when the mainstream press picked up the story. I was called for comment and interviewed on radio and television. I was even approached by a well-known radio station to debate the issue with the Net1 CEO. After initially agreeing, he never pitched up. The whole saga eventually resulted in the early retirement of the CEO and founder of Net1, albeit with an astronomical pay-out, and a complete restructure of the business. More importantly, the experience proved that shareholder activism can be deployed in a constructive way and that shareholders can be more than just passive passengers when it comes to influencing the strategy of a business. I wish more investment managers, as custodians of people's savings, would use their influence more aggressively to hold businesses to account. When I was at Coronation, the general mantra was that any criticism of a company must happen behind closed doors, otherwise the company's management would cut you off from receiving information. The Net1 story played itself out in front of all the analysts at all the investment management houses. Their silence was deafening.

There was worse to come. Soon after the social grants crisis, on 31 March 2017, Zuma fired finance minister Pravin Gordhan in a cabinet reshuffle that was seen as an attempt by the president to rid cabinet of his critics and once again gain control of National Treasury. Gordhan was on an international roadshow promoting South Africa to investors when news of his firing reached him. I will never forget the answer he gave when asked by journalists what average South Africans could do. 'What should the public do? Organise!' he said. A week later he gave a speech in Cape Town in which he called on South Africans to 'join the dots' in under-standing what was happening in the country. In response to his firing, the credit rating agencies Standard & Poor's and Fitch, international bodies that assess the risks and strengths of each country's economy and economic policies, downgraded South Africa's government bonds to junk status. This lower, 'below investment grade' rating meant the country had to pay even higher interest rates to borrow money, because, from an investor's perspective, the risk of lending money to an unstable and clearly corrupt government which could default on its debt repayments had increased.

Many foreign investors shy away from 'junk' bonds completely due to this higher risk.

I remembered how difficult it had been for South Africa to achieve its investment grade rating in 2000, and how we had all celebrated. I had been at an investment conference when the news broke, to general cheering. Zuma had destroyed all of that and more.

The downgrade was a wake-up call for big business. Business Leadership South Africa, an organisation that includes some of the largest and most influential companies in the country, took out a full-page ad in a leading Sunday newspaper calling on the ANC to vote Zuma out of power. The CEOs of many large South African corporates demanded a meeting with the president to discuss the irrevocable breakdown of trust between business and the government. Unfortunately, discussions about relationships are a bit like marriage counselling, lots of talking, cajoling and promising, but unless there is a real willingness by both parties to change and meet each other halfway, not much can be achieved.

April 2017 saw thousands of South Africans across the country joining mass demonstrations calling for Zuma to step down. Sygnia staff were given the option to participate if they wished. We came up with a well-organised plan, created a WhatsApp group to keep everyone safe, and printed blue T-shirts with the first names of well-known struggle icons and with 'Jacob' clearly crossed out. We turned placard making into a bit of a team-build and then marched from Sygnia's offices in Green Point to Parliament, where a large crowd had gathered. It was a joyful meeting of people from all walks of life united in a common purpose: getting rid of a clearly corrupt president. Unfortunately, not every corporate felt the way we did, with many employers refusing to give their staff the day off.

The press continued to publish allegations of government corruption and state capture, and many apolitical lobbying groups and civil society organisations joined the fight to expose the rot. Zuma's government parried these attacks with a narrative of radical economic transformation, white monopoly capital, land appropriation without compensation, nationalisation and racism. This divisive campaign emanated from UK-based PR firm

Bell Pottinger, which, as it later turned out, had been hired by Zuma's son Duduzane and the Guptas to seemingly distract and divert attention from their looting. Using Twitter bots and other media channels owned by the Guptas, the firm stirred up racial tensions in a toxic propaganda campaign that persists to this day. When their part in the affair came to light, Bell Pottinger was disgraced and ultimately went into liquidation.

After an initial, unsuccessful, meeting with Zuma in April 2017, big business just disappeared from the stage. I wrote several newspaper articles calling on business to take more active steps to hold Zuma and his government to account. I even published a list of steps that could be taken immediately to effect change, such as withholding capital by not buying government bonds, calling on the international investment community to stop propping up the South African government until corruption had been rooted out and proper governance restored, allowing staff to protest without deducting days from their leave, refusing to tender for government projects, suspending all projects managed for the government, donating more money to civil society organisations, trade unions and opposition parties to strengthen their campaigns for change, and lobbying foreign governments to exert diplomatic pressure on the South African government. In the battle of wallets, big business always wins. They were the only players that could have enforced real change. Unfortunately, they were nowhere to be seen.

I remember being taken to breakfast by a prominent business leader and being told that I was naive. 'Business swings with the wind,' he told me. 'If the environment encourages the payment of bribes to secure business, it will do so. If this practice is frowned on, it will stop.' Unfortunately, he's right. Most CEOs of large companies are employees. They are paid salaries and bonuses. They do not have the mandate to lead their companies on a crusade. Many rely on large contracts from government. The owners of the businesses, the often-anonymous shareholders, are unlikely to unite in giving them a mandate other than profit maximisation. I was in a different position, however. I ran my own business. I was not an 'employee'. I was not accountable to anyone. After my few previous brushes with corruption, I had no government clients. I was free to voice my opinions, and that is what I did. It set me apart from other executives and helped build my profile, but that is not what drove me. What drove me were the wasted opportunities to improve lives, the lunacy of a government focused on personal gain, and the bravery of ordinary people who stood up to the system and were subsequently abandoned by the corporate world. For me, standing up and speaking out, alongside journalists, non-profits and ordinary people, was not a choice, it was simply the right thing to do.

The Net1 saga and subsequent events raised my public profile. There were some advantages, but many more disadvantages. Suddenly everything I said and did was scrutinised, particularly by those who I'd crossed or exposed in the past. Articles were written about me, not about what I had to say. People thought they could take potshots at me because I didn't shy away from controversy, particularly when I believed I was acting in the best interests of our clients, or even a broader public. I have never sugar-coated anything I say, even if it causes offence. I have always maintained that people who disagree with me are welcome to debate the issue with me, but choosing to take offence and simply walking away is not good enough. I am not always right, and I am more than happy to backtrack and apologise if required should I lose a debate on facts.

Zuma and the ANC, perhaps predictably, did nothing in response to the protests and demands for change. Little did they know what was coming.

21

The GuptaLeaks

IN EARLY APRIL 2017, while the discontent was percolating, I was approached by the editor of an independent online newspaper, the *Daily Maverick*, to provide funding for the safe passage out of South Africa of a whistleblower who was in possession of a trove of emails that had the potential, I was told, to bring down the government of Jacob Zuma. He told me that the whistleblower required a substantial sum of money to leave the country immediately, as they believed their life was at risk. The urgency of the request motivated me to meet with the whistle-blower's lawyer, to whom I paid a retainer, trusting that in terms of legal professional privilege he would not disclose my identity. I would not have proceeded with the meeting had he not accepted the terms, as I did not want my involvement ever to be made public. The lawyer told me about the origins of the emails and asked for an immediate payment to secure the whistleblower's safe passage out of South Africa, emphasising that his client's life was in imminent danger and that they had to leave the country as soon as possible. I transferred the money there and then.

As discussions ensued, I began to suspect that the journalists saw the contents of the emails from a purely sensational reporting perspective. They contained explosive information that would ensure a steady stream of powerful articles over months, if not years. I warned them that I believed the information would have legal and political implications, and that the impact would be felt in South Africa for years to come. I told them that from my perspective they should release all the information as soon as possible, rather than spending months analysing it and writing piece-meal articles while South Africa burned. They ignored my concerns. For my protection, I kept a copy of everything. I also made an independent financial contribution to the newspaper's journalistic endeavours. All of this was done under 'deep cover', such was the level of fear at the time.

At the end of April, I received a message from a friend that there were rumours in Johannesburg that a cache of dangerous information about the Guptas was 'floating around' and was about to become public. It meant that people's lives were put at immediate risk. Concerned about my own involvement, I decided to seek legal advice. My lawyers advised me to obtain an affidavit from the whistleblower verifying how he or she came to be in possession of the information to preserve the chain of evidence. They also warned that I had probably only a couple of days before the Gupta family heard of my involvement and that it would be wise to safeguard my family. Senior counsel advised me that the best course of action to protect the lives of anyone who had knowledge of the data would be to release the information into the public domain as quickly as possible. My family and I left South Africa for the Maldives the next day and we stayed away until I could arrange personal security for us all.

In mid-May, I flew to London with a plan to 'democratise' the information as my lawyers had advised. By that stage, the whistleblower was meant to have left South Africa. Certainly, public knowledge of the existence of the data had put them in even greater danger. I contacted the International Consortium of Investigative Journalists in Sweden, who'd been involved in the Panama Papers the previous year, but they told me that analysing the data would take too much work. I considered WikiLeaks as an alternative but decided against it as it was too technically difficult to upload all the information. I eventually travelled to Paris to consult William Bourdon, a French lawyer who specialises in defending human rights. He is the founder of the Platform to Protect Whistleblowers in Africa, or PPLAAF, an organisation that assists and defends whistle-blowers whose disclosures are in the interests of Africa and litigates and advocates on their behalf. He too urged me to release the information as soon as possible and encouraged me to hand it over to those international authorities who documented crimes, and in particular money-laundering, spanning multiple jurisdictions. I did so, but I was very disappointed not to meet a real-life James Bond.

Based on all the advice I had received, I resorted to making multiple copies of the data for distribution. I spent five days in a hotel room in London, reading over 200 000 emails and classifying the most relevant into folders and storylines. I then made multiple copies of the storyline folders for distribution to recipients whom I believed would democratise the data by virtue of their senior positions, including heads of trade unions, heads of political parties, cabinet ministers and other public figures. My aim was to publicise the information as quickly as possible without endangering any lives. I did not send the information to any media outlets.

On 28 May, the *Sunday Times* and *City Press* newspapers, the largest news outlets in the country, published the first in a series of explosive articles based on 'damning emails' that showed 'the Guptas run South Africa'. The emails, the papers said, showed 'the extent of Gupta control over cabinet ministers and parastatal CEOs and board members' and gave 'insight into the role of Zuma's son Duduzane [a close Gupta associate] in presidential matters'. The press went into overdrive. A few days later, the *Daily Maverick* published an editorial in which they revealed that the Sunday papers had received only a fraction of the leaked data. They would now 'start publishing stories from a much, much wider trove'. And a trove it was. Christened the 'GuptaLeaks', the cache of emails and documents meant that no one could turn a blind eye to what was happening in South Africa any longer. While I had not sent the information to the newspapers directly, I had achieved my objective.

The events took a huge toll on me and my family. My older son had left to study in the United States, but my younger son had a bodyguard with him for the remaining two years of school. My own personal protection detail continues to this day. From my return to South Africa until Zuma resigned as president, my cellphone was tapped and I was followed by State Security agents. They would stop me at the airport every time I flew into South Africa and harass me for at least an hour. All of this was later confirmed by a Zuma-appointed State Security operative who testified at the Judicial Commission of Inquiry into Allegations of State Capture, better known as the Zondo Commission. I felt the full weight of social media abuse. I received death threats on Twitter. I was made into unpleasant memes. I was accused of involvement in prostitution. My name was linked to Polish assassin Janusz Waluś by Twitter bots. It was clear that I was on the radar. Whether it was a function of being outspoken or of my association with the GuptaLeaks, I will never know.

I never wanted my involvement to become public knowledge. I certainly did not anticipate the consequences. I am only writing about it now as the information has been put in the public domain by the whistleblower's lawyer, who broke client–lawyer privilege, as well as the journalists involved. But I do not regret my role. Some allegations have been made that I withdrew my support for the investigative efforts of the journalists. This is untrue. I was only ever approached to help the whistleblower. I tell this story reluctantly, knowing that my book would not be complete without my version of events. Everything I have written here is based on my sworn testimony before the Zondo Commission.

Sometimes, when you are presented with choices in life, all you have to go on is your gut feel for what is right or wrong. This was one of those situations. Did I weigh up the consequences at the time? Of course not. Did I examine all the risks? No. I did not consider the long-term impact this would have on my life. But it was, again, the right thing to do.

The GuptaLeaks brought the first tangible proof of just how corrupt the government had become. South Africans suddenly woke up to the fact that the costs of state capture were astronomical and mounting. Economic recession, credit rating downgrades, retrenchments, a volatile currency, the inability of SOEs and government to raise adequate funding, and higher interest rates on the funding they did manage to secure were taking their toll. It is alleged that the Guptas and their associates, including Zuma's son Duduzane, stole over R50 billion from South Africa and that the total cost of state capture exceeds R1 trillion. These are staggering figures.

Think of how many schools, low-cost houses and clinics could have been built with that money. All the debt of Eskom, the SOE responsible for the provision of electricity, could have been repaid four times over, allowing it to recover from mismanagement and prevent the load-shedding that has been crippling the economy for more than a decade.

Faced with the threat of becoming the next Zimbabwe, South Africans realised they needed to fight. While the relatively small population of our neighbour to the north had the option to migrate south, for South Africa there is no 'south' – there is only ocean. It was up to us to save ourselves.

One of the companies implicated in the GuptaLeaks was auditing firm KPMG, which had advised the Guptas for fifteen years since 2002. One accusation in the public domain was that KPMG, which was responsible for auditing Gupta-owned companies linked to money laundering, allowed the Guptas to treat the lavish Gupta family wedding as a business expense. Four KPMG partners attended the wedding. In 2015 KPMG also wrote a report which was used to discredit Pravin Gordhan, one of the strongest critics of the Guptas, by accusing him of setting up a rogue spy unit while he headed SARS. KPMG has since disavowed the report, but the damage it caused has been immense.

Based on this evidence, I fired KPMG as Sygnia's external auditors. Admittedly, having read the GuptaLeaks, I had more insight into their role than was then in the public domain. I called Trevor Hoole, the CEO of KPMG South Africa, into my boardroom to discuss his firm's relationship with the Guptas, as well as the SARS report. By that stage in my career, not many men regarded me as a dumb blonde, and even if they did, they usually changed their minds relatively quickly after meeting me. I don't think Hoole ever did. This despite me questioning him extensively on KPMG's role in enabling the Guptas to rob South Africa. His excuse was that he did not have any evidence, and even if there was evidence, it would take a long time to retrieve and analyse the data. He therefore had no immediate answers to give me. With a flair for the dramatic, I handed him a flash drive, telling him that I had done the work for him and that the drive contained all KPMG's documents and emails. He took it cautiously.

A few days later, I received an envelope containing the same flash drive and a letter from KPMG's lawyers advising me that they had not opened the drive and would not do so.

After Sygnia fired KPMG, other companies followed suit. But not enough. Some made excuses, others appointed additional auditors, but everyone was cautious. As the scandal unfolded, eight KPMG executives and partners, including Hoole, resigned. KPMG said it would donate R40 million it earned from auditing Gupta-linked companies, as well as R23 million it received for writing the 2015 report, to anti-corruption charities. They even met with me to ask what they should do to restore their reputation in South Africa.

As I have said, in most cases it is individuals and not companies that are at fault. In this case, the fault lay with the executive management team. Their action, and subsequent inaction, tainted the entire firm.

In August 2017, the opposition Democratic Alliance (DA) proposed a vote of no confidence in President Zuma. South Africans once again united, marching on Parliament in Cape Town where the vote was to take place. This time, we printed a few hundred white and blue balloons with the words 'Sygnia' on one side and 'Vote Country over Party' on the other. We carried them in bunches as we marched. Everyone we passed wanted a balloon, and we were more than happy to oblige. Soon the square in front of Parliament was a sea of blue and white balloons, calling for South Africa to unite against corruption. Unfortunately, despite several ANC parliamentarians breaking rank for the first time and voting against Zuma, like a cat with nine lives, he survived to fight another day.

But just as Zuma seemed untouchable, he was deposed as president of the ANC, and as de facto president of South Africa, by Cyril Ramaphosa at the party's December 2017 national conference. I played my part in raising funding for his campaign. There were so few options on the table, and I felt it was a make-or-break situation for South Africa. I am often asked what it takes to ensure an ethical government. My answer is simple. Begin with an honest president who has no incentive to steal. I didn't know

Cyril Ramaphosa. I had never met him. But the fact that he was independently wealthy was at least a start.

On the back of Zuma's ousting, investigations into corruption by multinational companies kicked into high gear. So many were implicated in paying bribes to the Guptas. From KPMG and the mighty management consulting firms McKinsey and Bain to the Bank of Baroda and HSBC, which allegedly enabled money laundering, and the German software provider SAP, the list went on. I remember being called by a non-executive director of SAP who had flown to South Africa to investigate allegations that executives on the ground had paid bribes to secure government contracts. Given how vocal I had become about corruption, she was calling me to explain SAP's side of the story. She told me that SAP was used to paying middlemen in many countries where they did business, but, given the bad publicity they were receiving in South Africa, they had decided to stop the practice in countries that fell below level fifty on the Corruption Perceptions Index, an independent measure of relative corruption across the globe. She lamented how much money this was going to cost them. I responded by asking: What did she want me to do, congratulate her? She said that she wanted me to have the full picture. I told her I now had the full picture and thanked her. I used this exchange in subsequent speeches on the topic of state capture. A few weeks passed before I received a phone call from an aggressive public relations woman hired by SAP. She said that SAP objected to the tone and manner in which I was repeating the contents of my conversation with the director. My utterances did not convey the spirit with which the disclosures were made, she said. Motivated by her rudeness, I tweeted the following on 24 July 2018:

Dear SAP. Next time one of your PR people phones me to lecture me on my tone and precise expression when talking about SAP paying off the Guptas I will make the recording public. I too tape my conversations. At least McKinsey paid back the money. Are you?

Given all that has come to light, we really cannot allow foreign investors to lay all the blame for corruption in South Africa at our door. Plenty of corporates in other countries participated in and enabled the looting of South Africa. None of these companies have been held to account by their respective regulatory bodies, despite all the evidence against them. At least when it came to light that bribes had been paid by multinationals in the arms deal in the 1990s, the UK and the US fined many of the companies involved. This time around, and despite all the evidence – including some multinationals paying back the money and thereby tacitly admitting to their role – no international regulator has done a thing.

In the months that followed, I wrote many articles in leading business publications to try to mobilise people to act. Sygnia even launched an anti-corruption campaign by offering to donate all management fees in respect of our money market fund to organisations fighting corruption. It is easy to blame big business for complacency, but even when we called on ordinary people to help, there was little take-up. It's like I said earlier: there are three groups of people in this world – those on one side who perpetrate crime, those on the other side who fight for justice, and a large portion in the middle who see nothing, hear nothing and do nothing.

In subsequent years, the GuptaLeaks have largely been overshadowed by the testimony of whistleblowers and witnesses at both the Commission of Inquiry into Allegations of Impropriety Regarding the Public Investment Corporation (PIC) and the Zondo Commission. The Guptas were merely at the top of the pyramid of corruption, fraud and injustice perpetrated against the people of South Africa. Since then, many more stories have made their way into the public domain. Unfortunately, to this day, the tide of corruption is threatening to engulf the country.

22

Whistleblowers and Commissions

ONE OF THE PRIVILEGES OF being identified as someone who stands against corruption is being approached by courageous whistle-blowers who do not know who to turn to. I have been contacted by several in the past few years. They are all my personal heroes and I salute them. For their safety, I cannot name them all, except for one who has since become a household name. Bianca Goodson was the CEO of Trillian Management Consulting, a consultancy and subsidiary of Trillian Capital Partners, a firm owned by Gupta associate Salim Essa. Bianca started noticing shady activities: the firm was using its connections to land lucrative government contracts, such as from Eskom, then handing them to external partners. In April 2016, after just a few months in her position, Bianca resigned and took the evidence with her. She was subsequently employed by the global accounting software company Sage. When she informed them of her intention to come forward with all the information in her possession and offered to resign if the company had any concerns about its reputation, her resignation was promptly accepted, as Sage seemingly feared any potential backlash. Apparently for big business, profit trumps truth every time. By this stage, Bianca had approached PPLAAF, and William Bourdon referred her to me for help.

When I met her in my hotel one evening in September 2017, she was petrified. She had given an interview to a newspaper about what she had in her possession, and it was to be published the next day. She had no protection against retribution. My first thought was to make her name public before she was exposed in the article. I made sure that the article mentioned that the data in her possession had already been passed on and I called all the radio stations proclaiming Bianca Goodson to be a hero. I hoped to protect her by relying on the theory that it is more difficult to get rid of someone in the public eye. I also offered her a job. She worked for us for a few months, but the events had taken an enormous toll on her health and personal life, and she left in 2018. I remember her telling me that she came forward despite everyone around her, including her closest family, trying to stop her. She remains in my thoughts, and I follow her on Twitter. She has since become an advocate for other whistleblowers.

I remember at the time thinking long and hard about the executives who run large companies in failing states. Did those in South Africa realise what was happening? Did they care? Was it business as usual? Did they think the economy would miraculously recover by itself? Did they think they were immune to the poverty around them, to the failing education system, to the rising crime rate? Perhaps they did. Perhaps 'white monopoly capital' is not about economic power lying in the hands of the few whites, but rather the complacency of many powerful white, and increasingly black, South Africans who still ignore the blatant inequality and do not hold government to account.

It is an indictment that the heroic whistleblowers who exposed the corrupt state were not the leaders of major corporations with unlimited resources at their disposal, but instead the ordinary people. Average people, leading normal lives, who were suddenly, unexpectedly, presented with the choice of doing the right thing or walking away. While 99.9 per cent of people would have chosen the latter, these brave men and women made the hard choices, choices that everyone, including their families, lawyers and even priests, advised against. Bianca Goodson, Mosilo Mothepu, the sources of the GuptaLeaks and the now-discredited KPMG report, the late Babita Deokaran, and others risked their lives and livelihoods to do what was right. Those whose names were made public were intimidated, threatened, harassed and spied on, as were the people and civil society organisations who stood up and supported them. I was fortunate in that I could hire bodyguards and lawyers, but for the majority who could not afford to do so, their actions took enormous courage. In most cases, they were driven by a strong moral compass and incredible bravery. Greater bravery than all those hiding behind corporate veils. I think it is crucial that we all do a lot more to celebrate the people around us who do the right thing. The people who publicly testified at the PIC and Zondo commissions of inquiry are no longer invisible. They walk among us. We owe some of them a big debt of gratitude.

I watched the televised proceedings of both commissions with fascination. One of my favourite theories at university was the prisoner's dilemma. Although taught as part of behavioural economics, it is premised on game theory and is a decision-making paradox illustrating that individuals making decisions in their own self-interest cannot achieve an optimal solution. Put another way, it demonstrates why two rational individuals might not cooperate, even if it appears that it is in their best interests to do so. It is 'every man for himself' behaviour.

The prisoner's dilemma was on full display at both the PIC and the Zondo commissions. While no doubt some of the perpetrators of state capture were driven by a real desire to confess and tell the truth, many were hoping to receive more lenient treatment in exchange for their testimony. Those in this latter group deserve little credit. They are not whistleblowers. They are merely performers in a play as old as time.

In my work with actual whistleblowers, I try to explain that they can do nothing about what happened in the past, but they can influence their own future. It is always better to come forward and tell the truth as soon as possible, rather than wait for someone else to do so. I encourage the same thinking in the organisations I lead. We're all human. I always assume that, at any given moment, someone is making an error, perhaps a big one. As I've said before, the problem is not the error itself, but rather hiding it. My only expectation is that they admit the mistake immediately and propose a solution. It is a philosophy that has worked well for me and for my staff.

After everything that's happened, I do ask myself whether there is a need for retribution. In June 2017, I wrote an article for a business publication titled 'We need another Truth and Reconciliation Commission'. The TRC was formed in 1995 to examine and help deal with what happened under apartheid. Victims and perpetrators of gross human rights violations were invited to testify before a tribunal to advance reconciliation and determine reparations. I remember it being a great cleansing experience. It nevertheless took a long time to translate into any real change in some of the accused. Adriaan Vlok, the former apartheid-era minister of law and order, only publicly apologised for his crimes in 2006. P.W. Botha, the former state president, never apologised and went to his grave unrepentant.

In many ways, the Zondo Commission, established in January 2018 to investigate allegations of state capture, was like the TRC. In a series of public hearings, the accused and their accusers were called to account and bear witness. Unfortunately, many of the perpetrators continued to lie and obfuscate about their respective roles in destroying the country. And none, like many of the perpetrators of apartheid, showed remorse. Whether any of these people will ever be prosecuted, one can only speculate. By 2022 the NPA was still investigating over sixty outstanding TRC cases, more than two decades after the commission released its final report. Similarly, I don't expect that the startling revelations contained in the Zondo reports will lead to any prosecutions any time soon.

I do not believe in wasting too much energy on looking backwards. There are too many perpetrators to believe that all of them will or can be prosecuted. It would take too long and cost too much. The best one can hope for is to see the main actors brought to book. The less-significant beneficiaries should be compelled to repay whatever bribes they accepted and then be let off. Companies should pass back their ill-gotten gains to the entities that were disadvantaged by the bribery and corruption. Some of the larger multinationals have already done so, but others hope that the issue will simply disappear and with it their involvement. But in the broader scheme, the Zondo Commission should have been viewed as a once-off cleansing to eradicate the rot that has eaten away at the moral fabric of South African society. It is unfortunate that the rot, rather than being eradicated, seems to be spreading.

Despite the litany of crimes on full display in front of the South African public, corruption intensified during the Covid-19 pandemic. More opportunities for profiteering and looting arose and the unscrupulous took full advantage. One such incident involved the national Department of Health. I had some dealings with them in early 2021 when I tried to help procure Covid-19 vaccines for South Africa. I had no personal financial interest in the transaction, but I did have access to the Serum Institute of India, one of the largest manufacturers of vaccines worldwide, and merely tried to make introductions. The people I dealt with were very 'nice' but completely and passively obstructive. Nothing progressed. Since then, several have been allegedly implicated, through commission or omission, in illegitimate tenders awarded during the pandemic. I suspect the reason my vaccine procurement discussions went nowhere was that I made for a poor middleman who would not pay or facilitate bribes.

Irrespective, as much as we may want vengeance, perhaps we should rather aim for a solution that could bring a swifter end to the economic collapse facing South Africa and allow us to heal and move forward in a constructive manner. I would rather focus on designing strategies for growing the economy, creating jobs, fixing the education system, addressing economic exclusion, attracting foreign investment, motivating domestic companies to invest, maintaining infrastructure, investing in renewable energy and the myriad other ways we can fix our society. I am not so naive that I think the current government, or any government that follows, will design and then adopt these policies on any grand national scale. There are some problems in South Africa that will not be resolved in our lifetime, if they are resolvable at all. I am rather talking about each person thinking about their scope of influence and doing their little bit to help. As for the major perpetrators of state capture, most of whom testified under duress, the fact that evidence given at the Zondo Commission can be used in criminal trials is a big step forward.

State capture has had consequences for the ANC. The party's support base is shrinking and may fall below the fifty per cent majority in the next national election. If it does, for the first time in many of our lifetimes, we may experience true democracy. But even then, the foundations are so weak that any coalition government that follows is likely to do as much harm as good.

23

Speaking Out

WHETHER YOU'RE A WHISTLEBLOWER or just someone who can't keep quiet when you see injustice, it is impossible to take on people involved in illegitimate activities without becoming a target. In 2017, when I started speaking out against Zuma, I placed myself in a precarious position.

In that year, I came under attack from one of Zuma's faithful supporters, his spokesperson Mzwanele Manyi. Manyi had allegedly entered a deal to 'buy' the Gupta-owned TV channel ANN7 and their newspaper *The New Age*, for R450 million. Both were used by the Guptas to spew divisive propaganda in support of Zuma. By that stage, all the banks in South Africa were refusing to deal with the Guptas, presumably making theft and money laundering more difficult. I suspected that Manyi was being used as a front to legitimise their continued business dealings. When I questioned the transaction and the source of his newfound wealth, Manyi took to Twitter, calling me a 'racist, hard at work to close down a black-owned platform'. He also compared Sygnia's staff marches against Zuma to 'terrorist activities'. In other tweets, and supported by an army of bots, I was told to go back to Poland, compared to Janusz Waluś and threatened with my life. I eventually had to take out an injunction against him.

Part 1 of the Zondo Commission report released on 4 January 2022 shed further light on Mzwanele Manyi. He was described by the commission as an 'enabler' of the capture of the state by Zuma and the Guptas as a consequence of spending over R8 million on advertising in *The New Age* between 2011 and 2012 while he was the chief executive of the Government Communication and Information System (GCIS). He had been appointed to the post while on suspension from the Department of Labour for disciplinary issues and after the former CEO was fired for resisting Zuma and the Guptas' demands to support the newly launched newspaper. When testifying before the commission, Manyi himself described the GCIS as the 'enabler department'.

As per the Zondo Commission report, 'one of the defining features that has emerged in the evidence before the Commission is that in order to divert public funds for private benefit, it was necessary to populate key institutions with people who were going to comply with orders'. Manyi was clearly one of these people.

During my frequent flights between Cape Town and Johannesburg, I was normally offered a choice of newspapers on board. I remember when *The New Age* became a paper of choice on both South African Airways and British Airways flights. When confronted with blatant fraud, I have a habit of loudly voicing my opinions. Whenever I was offered a *New Age*, I would ask the attendant why they were supporting corruption in South Africa. In most cases the stewardess would look embarrassed, as would the other passengers. In my opinion, there were many more 'enablers' – even if merely passively – of state capture than those named by the commission.

I did not limit my criticism to people linked to government corruption. In December 2017, South Africa was rocked by the biggest corporate failure on the JSE. Steinhoff, a darling of the investment management community, with a charismatic chief executive, announced that its auditors had refused to sign off on its financials. This shocked even the most seasoned investors, and Steinhoff's shares plummeted. Allegations of earnings manipulations, uncontrolled acquisition sprees and tax fraud followed. The warning signs were all there. Off-balance-sheet companies had been set up to hide losses, executives had collaborated to defraud investors, and debt had been taken on at a rapid pace. The most obvious was the cynical move by some individual shareholders, in a sleight of hand, to swap their shareholding in Steinhoff shares listed on the JSE in South Africa for a newly Frankfurt-listed Steinhoff, thereby externalising their wealth without the need for foreign exchange control approvals, a prerequisite for ordinary South Africans who want to invest their money directly offshore. Many big names were involved. Many people lost money. I don't feel sorry for those who, driven by a desire to externalise their wealth beyond South Africa's borders, overlooked red flags and had to deal with the consequences. I do feel sorry for the members of retirement funds and others who were unwitting investors and whose savings plunged as a result.

Steinhoff's failure was a pivotal moment for investment managers. Priding themselves on meticulous research, scrutiny of balance sheets and income statements, all backed by interviews with management, they should have seen the obvious: that this was as close to a corporate Ponzi scheme as one could get. When I looked at Steinhoff's financials, I had another Net1 moment. It took me one hour, perhaps two, to figure out the structural obfuscation, with financial items that made no sense, an acquisition spree that could not have been underpinned by any logic and was too frenzied to be well thought out, and debt levels that were out of control. I wrote a few articles on the topic.

A short while later, my phone buzzed with a WhatsApp message from my former Coronation chief executive telling me to check my inbox. It was the first time he had contacted me since I left Coronation in 2003. I opened the email to find threats of defamation lawsuits. I must admit I did not read the entire thing. He took exception to my articles about Steinhoff and my commentary about money being externalised. As it turned out, he had a significant personal investment in Steinhoff shares. He claimed that I had defamed him as he never externalised his shares and all his losses were made on the domestic stock exchange, the JSE. He attached his investment records as proof, inadvertently allowing me to establish that he had lost a large portion of the money he made from Coronation's listing, which he had clearly reinvested in Steinhoff at some stage. I believe that he had some protection against losses, but to me it was karma once again. I don't wish anyone ill and I don't bear grudges. I don't look backwards other than to search for learning opportunities. Life is too short for that. I do believe, however, that people's choices bring either good luck or misfortune, so choose wisely.

In 2018 I published an article about AYO Technology Solutions, a tech investment company largely seeded by the PIC on behalf of the Government Employees Pension Fund. By the time AYO caught my attention, journalists had already begun asking questions. Its financials made little sense. The PIC, on behalf of the pension fund, had invested at a ridiculous valuation into what appeared to be nothing more than an empty shell of a company with some potential deals in the making. AYO had also listed on the JSE on the unlikely date of 23 December 2017, when most of the investment management industry was on holiday. As it turned out, based on conclusions reached by the PIC Commission of Inquiry, the deal was highly questionable for several reasons, including allegations that governance and approval processes were deliberately manipulated and that AYO falsified aspects of its financial results. Further forensic investigation has been recommended, and the PIC has served AYO with a summons to pay back its R4.3 billion investment. Of course, none of this had come to light when I became the first prominent person to write about AYO.

As it so happened, via a web of companies and personal trusts, businessman Iqbal Survé had a large stake in AYO. Survé was best known in South Africa for purchasing the respected Independent Newspapers Group in 2013 with money borrowed from the same Government Employees Pension Fund, a loan that by 2018 appeared to have been written off without anyone knowing. I have always been advised not to take on anyone who buys ink by the barrel. The moment my AYO article appeared, Survé launched a vicious print media attack on me, publishing opinion pieces, which I believe were written by the chairwoman of AYO, calling me a 'subliminal racist' for daring to question the legitimacy of a black-owned company.

It is tragic that we live in a country where it is easy to shut down any criticism, however valid, by defaulting to racism. Unfortunately for Survé, words no longer hurt me, not after what I had experienced by then. They did, however, hurt Sygnia by association, and so I sued him and his newspapers for defamation, with those articles forming the basis of the proceedings. Given the slow pace of the South African court system, the court case will only be heard in October 2022. But that was not the end of it. After the listing of AYO, Survé attempted to list another – this time technically insolvent – company, and was once again supported by the Government Employees Pension Fund. I wrote another article, one voice among many, criticising the potential listing. Eventually, the JSE stopped the listing at the eleventh hour.

I had become an even bigger target. One hurdle I faced was that, at the time of Sygnia's listing on the JSE, and without knowing his reputation was sailing too close to the wind, I had allowed Survé to acquire an immaterial shareholding in the company. Now, given the animosity between us, I tried to negotiate the acquisition of his shareholding on behalf of an investor who had approached me with an offer. Even though he knew I was not asking to buy the shares for myself, Survé leapt at the opportunity to attack. Printing posters, hiring a spokesperson and using his brother-in-law as a proxy, he went as far as laying a criminal charge of attempted extortion against me. Of course, it went nowhere from a legal perspective and the Director of Public Prosecutions refused to prosecute, but it caused a lot of trouble with our clients, although admittedly most took the whole matter in their stride.

It is never pleasant to see your name in some scandalous headline. I sympathise with celebrities whose names feature prominently in the media. The idea that there is no such thing as bad press is a myth. Bad news sells better than good news, and nasty headlines lead to clicks. The only good that comes of negative publicity is that you learn to distinguish true friends from fake friends. The former will check up on you and express their support. The latter won't.

Undeterred by my brush with Survé, in 2019 I wrote an article for *Business Day* on the staggering 'advisory fees' paid by the PIC to various advisors in respect of transactions where the money invariably was lost or disappeared. I based my article on figures submitted to Parliament that had not found their way into the public domain until I highlighted them. As expected, there was outrage. Many of the details were subsequently investigated by the PIC Commission of Inquiry. One of the advisors I mentioned, Nana Sao, was unknown in South African advisory circles, and yet he had earned R64.2 million in fees. Lawyers representing Sao immediately wrote to *Business Day* demanding an apology under threat of suing the publication for defamation. I received similarly threatening emails. *Business Day* decided to comply, but I did not. What followed was a hilarious exchange of emails between me and Sao's lawyers, who continued to threaten me with a defamation lawsuit unless I apologised publicly. I continued to resist, both to issue an apology and to appoint lawyers to advise me, as they had suggested. By that stage I'd been exposed to enough defamation suits not to fear this one. The pestering eventually ceased after I wrote the following email to Sao's lawyers:

> Please stop this harassment or I will be forced to lay criminal charges against you for intimidation. If you want to sue me, please do so. I would welcome an opportunity to force your client to disclose every detail of his association with the PIC over many years and many transactions. The truth is always well worth the money, in my opinion, particularly in this situation where the monetary amount of a lawsuit will be negligible, while the truth priceless. I love a good forensic investigation and a lawsuit affords exactly that opportunity.

Sometimes you just need the courage to fight back.

I also took on the audit profession, an industry badly in need of reform. Several scandals have come to light in various jurisdictions in recent years, from Steinhoff in South Africa to Carillion in the UK and Wirecard in Germany. Auditors' lack of sufficient oversight and eagerness to comply with the demands of executives has practically given free rein to companies to perpetrate fraud. As mentioned earlier, I called out KPMG on the issues specific to South Africa. It was less of a campaign and more a request to do right by the shareholders who place so much faith in their audit reports, but it nevertheless made me very unpopular among auditors.

I also called out the JSE and their past executives for facilitating the controversial listing of companies such as AYO Technology Solutions and Oakbay, a company linked to the Guptas. I don't think the JSE had ever been tackled before; instead of looking at the merits of my questions, they did not take kindly to being quizzed. A number of JSE senior executives have since departed, perhaps due to their lack of oversight.

More recently, I criticised the Association for Savings and Investment South Africa (ASISA), a lobby group for large active investment managers whose aim was to block legislation that would have enabled South African investors to invest more money offshore. Several large investment managers persuaded ASISA to write a letter to National Treasury arguing against the legislation. The letter was only circulated to all members of ASISA after an internal whistleblower made me aware of its existence and I wrote to ASISA demanding sight of the letter. Before a letter of that nature was sent, all members of ASISA should have been consulted. Their motivation was clear. If investors took more money offshore, there would be less to manage domestically and hence their management fees and profits would be affected. I brought the issue to light and even wrote another of my forty-page proposals to the regulators, but it was too late. South African investors were betrayed by the very investment managers they trusted. Fortunately, in his 2022 Budget, minister of finance Enoch Godongwana, perhaps conscious of the arguments presented by both sides, partly relaxed foreign exchange control limits for retirement funds and other institutional investors.

Rightly or wrongly, my activist spirit has also seen me take on sectors beyond financial services, where I felt wrong decisions were being made. An example was the water crisis in Cape Town in 2018. The city was on the brink of disaster when the council called business leaders together to explain what contingency measures were in place. It soon became apparent that the contingency plan had massive holes in it. No one had considered how people would carry their daily allotment of twenty-five litres of water from the forty distribution points, that were still to be identified, to their homes. No one had considered how to get the water to the disabled and the elderly. No one had considered the need for vehicle access. I questioned all the measures in a public forum and was eventually invited to the city's committee meeting, which did not fill me with much confidence. What was even more absurd was being invited to a public debate with the Western Cape premier, Helen Zille, on the issue. I was not interested in a public debate on a topic I knew little about. And I am sure Helen had better ways to spend her time. All I wanted was to see realistic plans being put forward and the gaping holes in the strategy to be addressed. Fortunately for Cape Town and the city council, the rain came just in time.

I have paid a price for being controversial. Unsurprisingly, there has been pushback from the companies I have called out. For instance, I have been warned to stop scrutinising the audit profession or soon no auditor will accept a Sygnia appointment. It's a pity. When I appoint auditors, I always make it clear that I will never interfere in their work and that I am paying them to leave no stone unturned as I want to sleep at night knowing that Sygnia is run on a solid foundation. Besides the press, I have also come under intense scrutiny from the JSE. It's a price worth paying, though, even if I achieve nothing more than bringing issues into the public forum for discussion and debate. Hopefully, when confronted with any listing application, the JSE will look a lot closer at the proposal going forward.

When I get involved in something, I never claim to be an expert on the subject or that I can provide tangible solutions. It would be absurd to suggest that I believed I could solve Cape Town's water crisis or provide a framework for audit firms to monitor the work of their partners. I merely ask hopefully sensible questions to bring issues to the fore. I ask these questions because I care about the outcomes, and fortuitously have a public platform from which I can speak. I know that there are more qualified people who have the same and much better questions, but who have limited means to make themselves heard. Corporates, organisations and governments are composed of people who make decisions, some good, some bad. Individuals are thus responsible and should be held to account, rather than an amorphous entity such as an audit firm or a stock exchange.

To do otherwise would be extremely unfair to the 'good' people within those organisations who were not aware of the actions of others. Unfortunately, when 'bad' people are in executive positions, the entire firm is normally caught in the crosshairs, such as KPMG in South Africa.

When I look back at the things I have done, I recognise that in many cases I was caught up in the moment, my actions driven by moral indignation. On reflection, I could have done things with more finesse. I do not regret the steps I have taken, however. Someone had to do it.

24

Handing Over the Reins

I'VE HAD THE PRIVILEGE OF watching Sygnia grow from a fledgling company into a corporate player. However, as Simon and I still own over sixty per cent of the company, Sygnia remains a 'family' business. It took me a while to gather the courage to verbalise this, but it was important to do so. Family businesses are different to pure corporates and need to be managed as such. I have read widely on this topic. The *Harvard Business Review* has quoted a number of statistics that I find interesting. Family businesses, or companies in which two or more family members exercise control, represent an estimated eighty-five per cent of the world's companies. Family businesses are also the largest source of long-term employment in most countries. In the United States alone, they employ sixty per cent of workers and create seventy-eight per cent of new jobs. Their survival is thus essential to economic growth. Family businesses can be large or small, listed or private. Either way, they need to be managed with particular care so that they outlive their founders. Another statistic that I found in a Family Business Institute review is that thirty per cent of family businesses last into a second generation, twelve per cent remain viable into a third, and only three per cent operate into a fourth generation or beyond. That is a terrible strike rate, but it helped me recognise the need for good succession planning well in advance.

A few years ago, I read another article in the *Harvard Business Review* that talked about why so many family-managed businesses fail to thrive. Much can be attributed to the differences in the skill sets required to lead an organisation in the initial stages of its growth and to steer it when the organisation becomes bigger. The former requires more drive and passion, the ability to multitask and think creatively about products and services, and a willingness to pivot around market demand. The latter requires a rigorous approach to problem-solving, an organised business structure, supervision of risk and governance procedures, and creative thinking focused on execution. While some founders of businesses manage to transition from being entrepreneurs to being business leaders, many do not. Those that don't often fail to recognise when it is time to let go of the reins and allow professional executives to take over. There is strength in recognising which category you fit into. That article left a particular impression on me.

After all these years, I know my strengths and weaknesses. I am everything that an entrepreneur should be, but I possess none of the skills of a professional executive. This became apparent to me early in the Southern Life days. I am just not made for corporate life and for leading a corporation. As a company grows, its culture must shift. There comes a time when it is no longer appropriate to talk about the entrepreneurial spirit that drives the company. Instead, the focus should be on developing innovative growth strategies across multiple business lines, management of staff, soundness of IT and administration systems, designing a scalable client-servicing model and good governance, among others. When Sygnia was still a teenager, I had already begun letting go. I remember holding a strategy session with the executive team and giving them a lecture on responsibility and taking charge. I prohibited them from sending me emails on 'toilet paper' issues. I did not have any desire to micromanage. When Sygnia became an adult, I made the most difficult decision of my working career: to let go and allow Sygnia to soar.

To be honest, I had been preparing for the transition for a number of years. I knew early on that my sons were unlikely to enter the financial services industry. They have witnessed my struggles and they do not want to fight in that world. Understanding this, I began searching for a successor about a decade before. I identified a trusted and experienced friend, David Hufton, whom I had known for many years and in whom I had every confidence. It took five years to persuade him to join Sygnia, and another five for me to come to a point where I was completely comfortable to hand over the reins. In that time, he worked alongside me. After a while, I made him co-CEO so he could assume more operational responsibilities.

A year later, in May 2021, I stepped down as CEO and assumed the role of executive chairperson. It came as a shock to the market and the press. I think everyone expected me to die on the job, having built the company. I think most people do not understand entrepreneurs. There are many professional pseudo-entrepreneurs out there, those who have spun out businesses from within established corporates or who were backed by substantial capital. They never had to work for no pay. They never had to set up an office and buy every teaspoon and teacup themselves. They always had adequate resources. A real entrepreneur starts with nothing more than their own energy, brainpower and passion. Letting go of corporate responsibilities for a real entrepreneur is therefore easy. They are not our core strength. I believe that I have at least one, if not two different businesses in me yet. Sygnia will always be my third child, and I will remain fully involved in its strategy and direction. But my child has grown up. The time has come for it to thrive without me.

Of course, in a family business, one can never let go entirely. It is therefore important to have clearly defined lines of responsibility. I think assuming the position of executive chairperson is an elegant transition. It enables the founder to remain as involved as she or he wishes without stifling new management. In my new role, I am still able to contribute to setting Sygnia's business strategy.

After I stepped down as chief executive, a senior female colleague sent me the following email:

Years ago, I saw a woman in a man's industry achieving greatness – greatness that had to be built with years of hard work. I saw someone that spoke up against wrongs. I saw someone that stepped in for the greater good. I saw someone that had the ability to create something and to do it in a difficult environment. I saw someone that I wished I could be more like.

217

Today, I get to see from close. There are all the things that I saw from afar. I now also get to see someone that others rely on for insights. I see someone that works hard. I see someone that is open, someone that discusses and shares with ease. I see someone that is secure in themselves. I see someone that considers, covers angles and listens to others at the table (even when she is already ten steps ahead). I see someone that has a rare combination of qualities that makes her a natural leader in this world – someone that others want to follow, and for good reason.

You have strengths, ways of being and ways of working that make you exceptional. You are smart, you are clever, you are creative. You trust and you are trusted.

These are probably the kindest words I have ever read, and hopefully they are at least partly true. While I am aware that not everyone shares this view of me, it is a wonderful tribute to receive as I embark on yet another uncertain chapter of my life. It also says everything I want to say about what makes a good leader. Whether I have achieved all the above, I am not sure, but this email articulates exactly what leadership is all about. I could not have said it better myself.

Being a true leader, as opposed to a competent manager, requires a willingness to get your hands dirty. I have said before that I do not expect anyone to do a job I cannot do myself. While this is clearly unrealistic as a company grows and expands, the perception of being willing to step in and assist must remain. The weight of leadership includes staying calm while others panic and coming up with solutions rather than joining the chorus of complaints. The Covid-19 pandemic has certainly helped distinguish the leaders from the managers. Leaders are prepared to take responsibility when things go wrong, even if the true responsibility lies with someone else. Leaders are visible. Leaders have a vision, even if it is only short term. I don't really believe in long-term planning. I make up the rules of the game based on one-year plans. This means I always retain visibility and control. Five years is too long a time to have any certainty that the objectives will be met.

Leadership is not a popularity contest, but it also should not inspire fear. Leaders earn respect and loyalty, recognising that these take a long time to earn and a second to lose. A leader is not scared of collaboration and listening to the opinions of others, as well as accepting help when it's needed. Leadership is not a quality that you are born with, it is something that you learn over time. I was not a leader in my Coronation days, and I am the first to admit that I made a lot of mistakes. Even at African Harvest, as much as I achieved financial success and tried different techniques to earn respect, I never truly managed to deal with the unruly investment team. But, having built on years of experience, by the time I hit my stride at Sygnia, I was a leader.

Within any organisation of substantial size, there is space for more than one leader, whether they head up divisions or the organisation itself. There are several leaders across Sygnia weaving the fabric of our success. I am no longer the sole leader, having passed the baton on to others in pursuit of my own dreams. To quote the *Harvard Business Review*, 'The competencies most frequently required for success at the top of any sizable business include strategic orientation, market insight, results orientation, customer impact, collaboration and influence, organisational development, team leadership, and change leadership.' That is what I looked for in my successor, and that is what I found in David. I am confident that all the leaders I have groomed are more than capable of taking the company forwards.

25

What Does the Future Hold?

I AM BOTH EXCITED AND CONCERNED about the future. The recent pandemic has meant that many of our priorities have changed. It has demonstrated that the future belongs to innovation. Innovation in technology, healthcare, education and the workplace. Given that Africa has been left far behind the rest of the world in this area, that its population growth rates exceed those of developed markets, and that climate change is expected to affect Africa most severely, we should all be concerned. There are no easy answers, but unless we start debating the topic together, the future will remain uncertain.

South Africa is arguably living through its most challenging moment since P.W. Botha's infamous Rubicon speech in 1985. The narratives of white monopoly capital, radical economic transformation, land appropriation without compensation, nationalisation, attacks on the Constitution, and other obvious political sleights of hand have taken over from the urgent debates we should be having about economic growth, job creation and education.

In trying to figure out the future, I always refer back to Clem Sunter's 'high road' and 'low road' scenarios for South Africa. He gave a presentation at Pretoria High School for Girls many years ago and his analysis made a huge impression on me. As the country's most highly regarded scenario planner and strategist, hypothesising the future according to his framework is a useful start.

My high road scenario looks something like this: Businesses, civil society organisations, trade unions and opposition parties unite to take a stronger stand against the corruption within the current government and press for more and faster change. This strong, unified stand acts as a catalyst, forcing

221

the ANC's MPs and National Executive Committee to reconsider their choices and decisions and to vote the current corrupt structures out of power ahead of the 2024 national elections. New leaders rise within the party to 'recapture' the once-proud liberation movement. The ANC's policy of cadre deployment, which has already come under huge criticism and been a factor in the collapse of so many municipalities, ends. Yet despite the changes, the ANC loses its outright majority in the national elections, forcing political diversity at the highest levels of government. That diversity results in middle-of-the-road, pragmatic decisions, rather than adopting extreme left- or right-wing views. Strong boards of directors are appointed to lead SOEs, irrespective of race. National Treasury is once again staffed by experienced people with international credibility. The National Development Plan, or a version thereof, is finally implemented to jump-start the economy. The energy supply stabilises and renewable energy is embraced. Tax-free zones and other tax incentives attract foreign investors. South Africa opens its borders to skilled people from other countries. New plans are put in place to deal with inequality, including a renewed focus on the provision of relevant, accessible education for all. Universities are deployed as centres of innovation. Support for a strong judiciary continues. Freedom of the press is protected through ongoing financial support. Clawing our way out of junk status takes time, but with sufficient effort we eventually prove to the international community that South Africa is a worthy long-term investment destination, leading to faster growth and job creation. South Africa flourishes.

My low road scenario is not dramatic; it is merely a slow erosion of the economy, the Constitution, the judiciary and the free press. As the ANC focuses on factional infighting, corruption thrives and quality of life declines for all, but especially for the poor. Slowly, the rand decreases in value, inflation, taxes and interest rates rise, infrastructure deteriorates, and basic services decline in quality and quantity. Credit rating agencies continue to rate us as 'junk', forcing government to deflect money sorely needed by the economy towards servicing foreign debt. Foreign investment flows out of the country, the economy flatlines as corporate investment dries up, savings are worth less and corporate profits fall. Racial tensions increase as government continues to blame apartheid to detract attention from its own inattention to the plight of ordinary South Africans. The independence of the South African Reserve Bank is slowly eroded, unemployment and social unrest increase, government is unable to raise new funding, and the social welfare system, once a point of pride for the ANC, becomes unaffordable, leaving many more people destitute. The public healthcare system collapses, as does the education system, leaving another generation ill-equipped to deal with the challenges posed by the new technologies that are replacing manual labour. Crime rates increase and skilled people continue to emigrate, taking their talents and expertise with them. Everyone feels, and is, poorer. The ANC loses its majority, but is replaced by an equally corrupt or ineffectual coalition government, founded on unstable alliances and mixed policies, and likely including a limping ANC. Compromises are made about the future direction of the country, the steady decline continues and South Africa withers.

In 2017, I wrote an article titled 'The time to revisit the high road and low road scenarios' for a business newspaper. My high road scenario looked different then, as Zuma was still in power. But unfortunately, my low road scenario looked a lot like what has since transpired. On the balance of probabilities and based on what I see, I think we are continuing down the low road. I would, however, love to be proved wrong.

My extensive travels have enabled me to learn about and compare the economic and political trajectories of different countries. Perhaps it is apt to compare South Africa to Cambodia and Vietnam. Both Southeast Asian countries have managed to move on from their brutal past, which included colonialism, human rights abuses and internal wars. Our tour guide in Cambodia told us that everyone knew who the Khmer Rouge members were. They lived among them, as did Pol Pot, their ruthless leader who was responsible for killing close to a quarter of Cambodia's seven million people in an attempt to turn Cambodia into a communist peasant society. Those targeted were the educated middle classes, including anyone who wore glasses, which were interpreted as a sign of intelligence. After the fall of the Khmer Rouge, through a process of forgiveness and healing, the country managed to recover. After transitioning from a planned economy system to a market-driven one, the country started to attract foreign investment. Despite facing similar challenges to South Africa's, Cambodia's economy, largely driven by garment exports and tourism, has achieved one of the highest average annual growth rates in the world over the past two decades.

Vietnam was slightly different. After French occupation ended in 1954, the country was divided between the anti-communist South and the communist North. This ultimately resulted in the Vietnamese War, which led to American intervention. North Vietnam eventually won the war in 1975, brutally suppressing the South Vietnamese and imposing a communist regime on the country. A decade later, through reunification and a series of reforms, the Vietnamese managed to unite and thrive. Today Vietnam, similarly to Cambodia, is consistently ranked among the fastest-growing economies in the world.

It is a pity that South Africans cannot do the same. Racial divisions remain, encouraged by an inept government that continues to blame its own failures on the legacy of apartheid. At some stage, if we are to thrive, we need to follow the examples of Cambodia and Vietnam. We need to stop looking to the past and rather forge a better future, together. We cannot afford to be mere passengers any longer. We must actively choose the high road.

While the future of South Africa is difficult to predict, the future of the financial services industry is a lot more certain. The current generation of savers, the forty-plus-year-olds reared on the 'human touch' service proposition, is unlikely to make the switch to digital advice and will distrust algorithmic or artificial-intelligence-driven investment decision-making. They have been brought up on the reassurance of being told what to do by a person sitting across the table. They derive comfort from being in the hands of people they view as professionals and trustworthy. They believe that financial planning and investment management are extremely complex fields best left to experts.

By cloaking itself in a combination of complexity and obfuscation, supported by advertising professing almost mystical wisdom, expertise and skill, the financial services industry has fostered this dependency. A lack of transparency, unnecessary product complexity and made-up jargon have turned a fairly simple proposition into a potentially terrifying minefield of decisions that could mean the difference between prosperity and destitution.

The new generation of young savers, however, is different. They are being brought up on mobile connectivity, social networks, internet chat forums, online shopping, DIY knowledge acquisition, cryptocurrencies and instant push-of-a-button gratification. They are fearless, more educated, tech-savvy and much less 'human touch' dependent. They are also more used to making decisions, particularly in a gamified world. The recent trend to self-manage money, albeit amateurish in nature, emerged during the coronavirus pandemic with the popularity of the trading platform Robinhood and associated chat rooms. I have no doubt that this generational shift will shape the future of savings and investment, as well as financial advice. Super margins in an age of internet transparency and social connectivity are unlikely to be maintained. Transparency and connectivity will expose fees, educate consumers and simplify what is actually a very simple linear world made complex by the vested interests of financial services companies.

In fifteen years from now, the average, affordable laptop is expected to pass the Turing test, the point at which a machine can exhibit intelligent behaviour equivalent to, and indistinguishable from, that of a human. Once that happens, and together with other advancements in artificial intelligence and virtual personal assistants, people will be able to interact with their computers as they would with human beings, asking questions and receiving accurate answers. Combine this with instant access to financial products and the demand for extensive human-driven services will reduce drastically. Although demand for 'human touch' will continue from those reared on it, for the rest, advice sought online from 'trusted advisors', in whatever form they come, will start to dominate. A trusted advisor will remain human, but it will be someone who is recognised and validated by others as an expert in the field and who provides generally applicable advice in a digital form only. Mobile applications will support micro-investing, where it does not matter how much or how little you have to save. Other fintech innovations, including blockchain and smart contracts, will make transacting instant and cheap. The financial services industry as we know it will cease to exist. This is particularly true of investment management.

Supported by advances in artificial intelligence and machine learning, algorithmic investment management processes will take over what wealthy, but short-sighted, investment managers do today. This is already visible in the stockbroking industry – the interface between investment managers and the stock market – which is crumbling both in terms of employment opportunities and profitability, with most trading now being driven by cost-efficient algorithms. Investment management of listed stocks and bonds will become a cheap commodity as similar algorithms replace overpaid investment managers in decision-making. It is highly likely that emotionless mathematical and statistical equations, processing massive amounts of data objectively and at lightning speed, will make better decisions. The differentiation in investment returns will be premised solely on who builds the better mousetrap. Once built, there will be no need for people.

Performance-seeking, sophisticated investors will shift their focus to investing in start-up ventures and private companies. Change happens faster than one expects.

Sygnia was the first company in South Africa to launch a robo-advisor, a web-based tool that assists investors in making investment decisions. I am the first to admit it has been a failure to date. But that is not to say it will not succeed in future. Even in their current 'unsophisticated' form, robo-advisors offer simplicity, convenience and affordability. A robo-advisor does not care how much money you make or how you make it, what you look like, where you live or what your financial prospects are. It does not need you to set up an appointment. It is available 24/7 to suit your schedule. The current generation of robo-advisors will evolve to include speech recognition and human-like interaction. They may only ever remain just one of the tools used by investors, but they already provide a glimpse of the future.

And what does the future hold for me? Stepping down as CEO of Sygnia opened a host of new avenues for growth and experimentation. I had always lived and worked in South Africa and never really challenged myself on the global stage or experienced living overseas. Intuitively, I knew that my next business venture would need to be outside the country. It would involve learning about the broader world of opportunities, as well as a bit of experimenting. You do not always get it right on your first try, but even if it remains an experiment that never makes its way out of the laboratory, it is a great knowledge-acquisition strategy.

I am and remain an entrepreneur and business builder, and was already on the lookout for another opportunity as I prepared to hand over Sygnia. With a highly knowledgeable and experienced partner, we set up an advisory firm in London specialising in the management of venture capital funds. While far removed from what I am used to, I believe venture capital management is the only type of investing that will thrive in the future. Venture capital firms invest in start-ups in the unlisted space. These are basically the businesses of the future. Start-ups require a completely different skill set. Their founders begin with an idea, but have little experience in how to turn that idea into the reality of a company worthy of attracting investors. Moreover, they lack the skills to commercialise their idea. This is where venture capital firms step in. They invest in the start-up, providing much needed initial capital in exchange for a stake in the business. They also help set up the business, guiding the founders in, for example, hiring the right management teams. To be honest, investing in start-ups is hit and miss. Some will succeed beyond your wildest expectations, but many will fail. However, from an investor's perspective, you only need two or three successes to make a lot of money. Venture capitalists only get to invest in ready-made entrepreneurs if they are lucky and are approached by those entrepreneurs. Usually, however, it's fairly naive people with good ideas. This is not a problem, but it seldom breeds true entrepreneurs, as over time the successive rounds of capital raising to continue operating mean that the founder's shareholding reduces massively, while those funding the business grow their stake and ultimately take control of the company.

Being involved in making decisions as to which start-up to support financially comes more naturally to me than making educated guesses as to the direction of listed markets swayed by sentiment and daily news as much as anything else. Given my commercial experience, I know what it takes to build a successful business and hopefully look at the opportunities available to us through that lens. I am also, for the first time, working with an equal partner in a business venture. It is a very different dynamic to flying solo, but one that, fortunately, I have become accustomed to while working with David as my co-CEO of Sygnia.

It took us two years to set up Braavos Investment Advisers in the UK. I was effectively holding down two jobs, being co-chief executive of Sygnia and a multitasking entrepreneur at Braavos. Just as the business was up and running, the pandemic hit. For me it turned out to be a mixed blessing. Having set up two venture capital funds, we needed to find investors who would trust us with their savings. In a normal world, I would have packed my suitcase, made appointments, boarded a flight and tried to sell the new proposition to largely institutional investors. The pandemic made that impossible. We were in lockdown in our Cape Town apartment with our two sons. But innovative teleconferencing programs such as Zoom and Microsoft Teams provided an opportunity to engage with a wider audience virtually.

Our investment proposition was sufficiently attractive for many institutional and some retail investors to commit over R6 billion to the venture. Setting up a venture capital business exposed me to a different world, a world where money for people with ideas is plentiful, where firms and wealthy individuals are prepared to take risks and back small businesses, and where the founders do not have to struggle like I did. It also made me aware that nothing like that exists in South Africa. We have a lot of smart people with a lot of innovative ideas. Without capital, however, they either leave South Africa to pursue opportunities overseas or they allow their dreams to die. With what I've learnt over the past two years, I would like to, in time, bring the venture capital industry to South Africa, even if merely through a skills transfer process.

The early success of Braavos's venture capital funds meant that remaining an active co-CEO of Sygnia was unfair to the company and, more importantly, to the people I had groomed over the years to take over. It was therefore another reason to step down as a CEO and become an executive chair. It is the best of both worlds, and I'm excited about my future. I am still involved in strategically managing Sygnia, and scouting for opportunities for the business offshore, and I look forward to what we can achieve with Braavos. I give guest lectures at Columbia Business School in New York, in which I try to pass on some of the lessons I have learnt. I sit on some advisory boards in the US, which give me another reason to travel and see my sons. Simon and I recently celebrated our twenty-fifth wedding anniversary. And, of course, I have written this book.

I was recently asked if I have enjoyed my life. It's a tough question to answer, but I think I can sum it up like this: I believe that my life chose me, rather than the other way round. Many of the things that happened to me were outside my control. Those that I could control were a function of the experiences I'd had. I was very young to be given the kinds of responsibilities that I was given at Coronation and African Harvest, but the way I see it, my age was not determined by the date on my birth certificate, but rather by having to become an adult at the age of twelve when my family arrived in South Africa. I had a good ten years on many of my contemporaries. I'm not bitter about this. It's my experiences that have got me to a place where I can begin to make a difference in people's lives. And if I have one overarching objective in life, it's to be remembered as someone who made a difference.

229

Acknowledgements

THERE ARE A LOT OF people who have helped me on my journey. I couldn't mention all of them in these pages, but I would not be where I am today without their help and their belief in me. This book would not be complete without acknowledgement of their immense contribution to my success.

First and foremost, to my closest family, Simon, Nick and Alex, your support over the years, and the personal sacrifices you have made to let me flourish, are what has allowed me to succeed beyond my wildest expectations.

To my mum and dad, thank you for sacrificing your own lives to ensure that I had a chance at a life free from oppression. Thank you for instilling in me the values of hard work, compassion for others and a moral compass that guides everything I do.

To my brother Wojtek, sister Ashka and sister-in-law Trish, words can't express how grateful I am to have you in my life. Your support and your dedication to Sygnia today motivate me to go on.

To the entire team at Penguin Random House who, for a first-time author, made the experience seamless, professional and enjoyable. In particular, I want to thank Marida Fitzpatrick who did not give up until she had persuaded me to write my story, and Bronwen Maynier and Robert Plummer who spent hours shaping a raw manuscript into a book I am proud of.

To Willem van der Merwe, your energy, incredible skill set and tireless determination to make Coronation, IQvest, African Harvest and Sygnia a success have been an inspiration.

To Joseph Potgieter, you are a genius. Sygnia would not be Sygnia without you.

To Niki Giles, you are an inspiration who sets an example to all women who follow in your footsteps. Thank you for what you have done for me over the years. Your 'What are we all doing next?' question sparked an idea that turned into a whole business.

To Mzi Khumalo, who gave a young, inexperienced woman a chance, an extraordinary gesture that became the foundation for all that I have been able to achieve since.

To Professor Haroon Bhorat, thank you for being a listening ear whenever I need it. Your wisdom and guidance are invaluable. You have chaired Sygnia's board for many years and have steered the ship through many a rocky moment. I want to specifically thank you on my behalf, and on behalf of many others, for the immense, often non-public contribution you have made to fighting state capture.

To Iain Anderson, my first ever employee, you have always been there, supportive, kind and caring throughout my entire working career. You have built teams that in turn have helped me build companies.

To David Hufton, you have courageously taken on the challenge of following in my footsteps. I knew I had chosen well years ago when I first tried to persuade you to join Sygnia. It took a while, but you are finally where you belong, and I know Sygnia is in safe hands.

To all the whistleblowers who I cannot name, thank you for coming to me and trusting me to help you through your most difficult hour.

To all my friends who have been there since the beginning and who wanted nothing from me over the years but friendship.

To all the leaders of financial services groups who have supported me and believed in me through many years of turbulence. Your faith in me, despite some of the craziness that I seem to attract, is what has been and continues to be a large part of my story.

To all the clients who trusted me to manage their money, from the days of Coronation, through IQvest, African Harvest, Sygnia and finally Braavos. Everything I have been able to accomplish is a function of that trust.

ACKNOWLEDGEMENTS

To all the people who have worked alongside me and for me, thank you for allowing me to be a leader.

MAGDA WIERZYCKA
CAPE TOWN
MARCH 2022

Index